*Life*Topics

W9-BHS-961

Contents

*Life*Topics

Stress Fractures

Charles R. Swindoll

Adapted for Group Study by
Jan Johnson

David C. Cook Publishing Co., Elgin, Illinois—Weston, Ontario

Stress Fractures
A LifeTopics Study

LifeTopics study version © 1991 David C. Cook Publishing Co.

Stress Fractures by Charles R. Swindoll, upon which this course is based, © 1990 by Charles R. Swindoll, Inc., and published by Multnomah Press, Portland, OR 97266

Unless otherwise indicated, all Scripture references are from the New American Standard Bible, © The Lockman Foundation 1960, 1962, 1963, 1968, 1971, 1972, 1973, 1975, 1977. Used by permission.

Published by David C. Cook Publishing Co.
850 North Grove Ave., Elgin, IL 60120
Cable address: DCCOOK
Designed and illustrated by Bob Fuller
Printed in U.S.A.

ISBN: 1-55513-564-1

Welcome to LifeTopics

Congratulations! You're about to accomplish an amazing feat. And, thanks to this book, it's going to be easier than ever.

You're about to bring key concepts from an outstanding Christian book to a group study setting. You're going to make a book into an active, life-changing group experience.

We've turned Charles R. Swindoll's *Stress Fractures* (published by Multnomah Press) into a 13-week course for adults. With this LifeTopics study, it is not necessary to buy a copy of *Stress Fractures* for each group member. That's because this course uses short, reproducible book excerpts and creative group activities to communicate vital principles from the original book. If you and your group would like even more insights, however, we encourage you to purchase the original *Stress Fractures* as a supplement.

These 45-60-minute sessions are easy to follow and to lead. Instructions to you are in regular type. Things you might say aloud to the group are in bold. Suggested answers are in parentheses.

Each session is accompanied by reproducible Resource sheets. Some of them are excerpts from the original book. Some are creative group exercises. Some you'll want to photocopy and hand out; others you may want to turn into overhead transparencies. The session plans spell out how to use each Resource.

Whether you lead a large Sunday school class, a small group, a home Bible study, a midweek meeting, or another group, you'll find it easy to bring this book to life. Get ready for lively sessions, solid biblical principles, and specific life application. That's the LifeTopics way of learning.

John Duckworth, Series Editor

Introduction

Consult a medical book, and it will tell you that stress fractures have to do with microscopic cracks in bones. Consult an engineering manual, and it will tell you that stress fractures have to do with hidden, hairline fissures in bridges and pillars and foundations. Consult your daily life, however, and you'll acknowledge that the constant stress and pressure you've been enduring has produced fractures of an entirely different sort.

You're hurting, and you can't explain why.

You have wounds, but you couldn't say where.

You're desperate for help and healing, but you have no idea where to find it. . . .

Stress fractures.

. . . Breaks in bones are painful, but can they match the ache of a fractured spirit . . . or a broken heart? Perhaps you've felt that kind of pain recently. A pain that lies deep. A pain that haunts you through the day and throbs into the night. . . .

Let me pass along some good news. Your stress fractures don't have to go on hurting. You don't have to turn to noise, drugs, alcohol, or an extra-marital affair to cope with the pressure you've been enduring. You don't have to push yourself until something snaps with a sickening crack.

This book has some answers that *cannot fail* to bring you relief. I make that statement with confidence, not because of this author's ability, but because of the unfailing, infallible source from which I draw. I speak of our great and gracious God and His eternal Word, the Bible.

—*Chuck Swindoll*

(Excerpted by permission from *Stress Fractures,* © by Charles R. Swindoll, Inc., and published by Multnomah Press.)

STRESS

Session 1

Whoever dubbed our times "The Aspirin Age" didn't miss it very far. It is correct to assume there has never been a more stress-ridden society than ours. For many, gone are the days of enjoying bubbling brooks along winding pathways or taking long strolls near the beach. The relaxed bike ride through the local park has been replaced with the roar of a motorcycle whipping through busy traffic. The easy-come, easy-go lifestyle of the farm has been preempted by a hectic urban family going in six different directions . . . existing on instant dinners, shouting matches, strained relationships, too little sleep, and too much television.

Add financial setbacks, failure at school, unanswered letters, obesity, loneliness, a ringing telephone, unplanned pregnancies, fear of cancer, misunderstanding, materialism, alcoholism, drugs and an occasional death; then subtract the support of the family unit, divide by dozens of opinions, multiply by 365 days a year, and you have the makings of madness! Stress has become a way of life; it is the rule rather than the exception.

—Chuck Swindoll

YOU'RE AIMING TO . . .
- Help group members identify with stressed-out biblical characters and understand biblical principles of handling stress.

YOU'LL STUDY . . .
- Luke 10:38-42; Exodus 18:13-26; I Samuel 30:6
- Major themes from Chapter 1 of the book, *Stress Fractures*

YOU'LL NEED . . .
- Copies of Resource 1A, "A Terrible, Horrible, Very Bad Day"
- Copies of Resource 1B, "Shifting the Stress by Prayer"
- Pencils
- Chalkboard and chalk or newsprint and marker
- Copies of Resource 2B, "Peace in Action" (optional)
- Bibles

Step 1 *(5-7 minutes)*

Troubles for Tyler
Recalling the Stresses That Drain Us

Hand out copies of "A Terrible, Horrible, Very Bad Day" (Resource 1A) and ask group members to form smaller groups of four or fewer.

Direct people's attention to the top portion and say: **Do you ever feel sad, tense, or embarrassed for your favorite television or book character? You're supposed to. The writer puts these characters in embarrassing or difficult situations so that you, the viewer or reader, will want to know how he or she will get out of it.**

Today you have a chance to create tough situations for a typical leading man we'll call Tyler. Complete at least five of the ten sentences with situations that annoy and frustrate you. Make these situations as stressful as you like; you won't have to come up with the solutions later!

After people have had time to work, ask each small group to share two entries. Ask each group if anyone in it has had that stressful event happen to him or her. Ask people to keep Resource 1A since they'll be using it again later.

We're all stressed by various situations. Today we'll see how a godly man and woman handled their stress.

Step 2 *(20-25 minutes)*

Heroes Get Stressed, Too
Seeing How Some Biblical Heroes Handled Stress

Write the following two names, descriptions, and references on the chalkboard or newsprint. Each group member should choose which one more closely resembles his or her own identity when under stress. Have each person find a partner to work with who has chosen the same character.

Type 1: Martha, the Overcommitted Superperson (Luke 10:38-42)

Type 2: Moses, the "Lone Ranger" Leader (Exodus 18:13-26)

Write the following questions on the chalkboard or newsprint. Ask the pairs to look up the passages and answer these questions about their characters.

a. What did this character do to deserve this title?

b. What did this character do to relieve the stress? (Concerning Martha: What should she have done?) Be as specific as possible.

Allow group members a few minutes to work on this. Then ask for their feedback. Use the following information and questions as needed.

Martha

(Martha tried to do so much so perfectly that she became a martyr of sorts. To relieve the stress she complained, blamed and manipulated.)

Chuck Swindoll comments on Martha's actions:
- "She assumed the Lord Jesus didn't care—'Lord, do You not care . . . ?'
- She blamed Mary for being irresponsible—'. . . my sister has left me to do all the serving alone . . .'
- She tried to work things out her way—'. . . tell her to help me.'"

Ask the entire group: **Why do we sometimes assume that Jesus doesn't care?** (We might assume that God only works through activities or relationships that work perfectly. Yet God actually can use informal, half-baked efforts and even hardships.)

Swindoll says that Martha was "active, energetic, diligent, thoughtful, and determined. . . . But her problem grew out of hand when she attempted to do more than was necessary." We find ourselves doing more than necessary when we want to impress others. When does that happen to you? (When we host people in our homes; when we're completing a high-profile job our supervisors are concerned about; when we want our children to be noticed, we force them to do more than is necessary, too.)

Martha seemed to be pulled in different directions. What causes us to be that way? (Being unsure of our priorities; competing with co-workers, friends, parents of our children's friends; being overcommitted.)

Moses

(Moses tried to do all the judging himself. His father-in-law explained how he should appoint others so he could spread out the workload. Moses wisely did so.)

Ask Type 2 people: **Did Moses complain to Jethro or did Jethro come to Moses? What does this suggest?** (Moses didn't complain; it was Jethro who said that Moses would get worn out [vss. 17, 18]. Chuck Swindoll describes Moses as a "workaholic." Perhaps Moses liked having too much to do.)

Did Moses back off completely? (Moses decided only the difficult cases [vs. 22].)

Ask the entire group: **What kind of pattern does this suggest for those of us who are overcommitted?** (If we are doing a job that someone else can do, we should give it away as much as possible. If we're doing something that we are uniquely able to do, we should continue that job—and only that job.)

Ask Type 2 people: **Workaholics often complain that no one else is qualified. How did Jethro address this issue before it was even asked?** (He said Moses should first teach the people the laws. Then he should choose capable men from the people.)

Ask the entire group: **How much of Martha's stress did she create for herself?** (Martha created most of her own stress by trying so hard to be a good hostess.)

How much stress did Moses create for himself? (Moses' problem began because so many people needed a judge; he added to it by trying to judge them all himself; he eliminated it when he so quickly followed his father-in-law's advice.)

Step 3 *(10-15 minutes)*

From Adventure to Melodrama
Looking at How Prayer Relieves Stress

Pass out "Shifting the Stress by Prayer" (Resource 1B). Ask group members to read the upper portion.

Then ask them to print an asterisk at the point when the narrative stops being an "action-adventure" story and turns into a "devotional melodrama." (Most will probably mark the space before the last sentence of the Scripture quote, after "his daughters.")

David did eventually rally his men because they regained their families and defeated the Amalekites, according to I Samuel 30:17-20. The turnaround point for David and his men was prayer. This is awfully different from the action adventure movies of today, isn't it? It almost seems too easy.

Redirect the group's attention to the lower portion of Resource 1B, "The Rest Available Today." **Let's figure out how these principles actually work. Let's say that Linda is a single mom who has just enough money to pay her rent and buy food for two weeks. Let's walk her through these steps to see how they would work.**

Ask the following questions as you work through the steps.

Step 1: **But what if Linda hears that there will be a going-away luncheon for a co-worker in two weeks for which she needs $10?** (Keep acknowledging God's control. It's no use to worry until she's asked for the $10. God may change the circumstances by then.)

Step 2: **What specific biblical promises can Linda claim about finances? About single parenting?** ("And my God shall supply all your needs according to His riches in glory in Christ Jesus" [Philippians 4:19]. "He [the Lord] supports the fatherless and the widow" [Psalm 146:9].)

Step 4: **What are some specific (and cost-free!) ways that Linda can "rest" instead of worrying?** (Prayer, of course—and taking a bath, reading a library book, or taking a walk.)

Step 5: **What can Linda say to a friend who says, "What are you going to do if after two weeks you don't have any money?"** (Explain that she will continue to trust God, rest in Him, and claim His promises.)

Step 4 *(15-20 minutes)*

Stress Strategies
Seeing How These Methods Work Today

Ask group members to help you list areas in which stress often occurs in our culture. Write these areas on the chalkboard or newsprint. Add these if they're omitted: financial pressures; raising children; couples spending time together; staying physically fit; resolving problems of our past; maintaining a home; completing our tasks at work.

Then ask people to team up with their partners again. **Choose one of these areas and create a story in which a person feels stressed in that area. Have your character handle the stress by changing an attitude, delegating some jobs, or "shifting the stress by prayer." Be ready to tell the group your stories.**

If time doesn't allow the group to come up with stories, just use the two that follow.

1. On the stress of maintaining a home: Julia felt overwhelmed trying to keep her house clean. So she delegated vacuuming and cleaning the bathrooms to her children. They didn't do it perfectly, and there were times when someone stopped by that Julia eyed a piece of dry cereal that had been left under the dining room table. But her Saturdays were much more relaxed.

2. On the stress of completing our tasks at work: Steve's job was becoming so full of pressure that he worked through lunch time. He began dreaming about the stress of his work every night. To lessen the stress, he decided to take his full lunch hour, using the second half as time to read the Bible and a short devotional book in the park every day. He arrived back at work with more energy and a better attitude toward fellow workers. It seemed he was getting just as much done, and he was sleeping better.

Neither of these solutions is perfect or dramatically wonderful. Each is a small step that can make things better.

If people have come up with their own stories, ask them to share. Encourage other group members to suggest solutions for the characters in the stories, too.

These principles—delegation, heart-felt prayer, re-thinking our priorities—aren't new to us. We know them, but we don't put them into action. Why?

Allow people time to think about this. (It takes time to train people; we think we're the only ones who can do it right; we want everything perfect.)

Many of us, like Martha, blame and complain instead of solving problems. We don't take time to consult with God, who can provide the motivation and conviction to change.

Step 5 (5-7 minutes)

When Perfectionism Isn't Perfect
Giving Our Incomplete Tasks to God

Direct the group's attention to "The Perspective of Jesus" on Resource 1A. Read it individually or aloud.

We can avoid getting stressed out by "terrible, horrible, very bad days" when we align our expectations with God's expectations. We need to release our grip on all the details.

What tasks are you no longer going to try to do a perfect job of completing? Being the perfect worker on your job? Being the perfect parent? Having an immaculately clean home? Moving to a bigger and better neighborhood? Being "super spiritual"?

Ask people to consider their answers to these questions. Then have them share with one other person how they would finish the following sentence:

"I need to release my grip on the following details . . ."

Optional: Before group members leave, pass out copies of "Peace in Action" (Resource 2B). Encourage them to read the sheet this week in preparation for the next session.

A TERRIBLE, HORRIBLE, VERY BAD DAY

PART 1: CREATING IT

1. Tyler woke up Monday morning, looked in the bathroom mirror, and saw to his horror that . . .

2. Tyler got out his work clothes and noticed . . .

3. As Tyler sat down to eat his breakfast, he looked at his chair and . . .

4. Tyler waved good-bye to his kids and noticed . . .

5. When Tyler got out to his car . . .

6. When Tyler got to work, he opened his briefcase to find . . .

7. When Tyler arrived home, he greeted his wife to discover that . . .

8. Tyler then opened his bank statement to find . . .

9. Tyler opened a card from his mother and remembered . . .

10. Tyler sat down to relax, but . . .

PART 2: AVOIDING IT

THE PERSPECTIVE OF JESUS

The night Jesus was placed under arrest, . . . He had been praying to the Father. In that prayer, He said: "I glorified Thee on the earth, having accomplished the work which Thou hast given Me to do" (John 17:4).

When you think that through, you will be surprised. He said that He had completed the job. Mission accomplished. Yet there were still regions which had not heard. There were still hundreds of blind and sick and lame people as yet untouched and unchanged. There were still millions of slaves in the Roman Empire being mistreated. Yet He said He had accomplished what the Father had for Him to do. Even though there were still numerous needs, our Savior was free of stress. Unlike His nervous friend Martha, Jesus maintained the right perspective.

—*Chuck Swindoll*

SHIFTING THE STRESS BY PRAYER

by Chuck Swindoll

Prayer is another relief—an essential therapy during stressful times. I'm reminded of David on one occasion. He and a group of his men returned home after a weary three-day journey. They found that while they were away, an enemy tribe had made a raid on their homes and had burned them to the ground. On top of that, their wives and children had been taken captive by the enemy. It wasn't very long before their morale hit bottom. . . .

. . . To make matters even worse, mutiny broke out. The men spoke of stoning David because they were embittered against him. They indirectly blamed their leader for what was happening.

"Moreover David was greatly distressed because the people spoke of stoning him, for all the people were embittered, each one because of his sons and his daughters. But David strengthened himself in the Lord his God" [I Samuel 30:6].

. . . He [David] got alone and prayed. He shifted the pressure from his own shoulders to Jehovah's. He knew that the stress was too big a load for him to carry alone, so he "trusted in the Lord with all his heart," and God immediately began to push away the obstacles. . . .

The Rest Available Today

God continues to hold out to all His children a peaceful, worry-free lifestyle that we can enter into on a moment-by-moment basis.

Will it happen automatically? No, we are instructed to "be diligent to enter that rest." [Hebrews 4:11] What does that mean? Simply this:

1. We acknowledge that our God is in full control of our lives. No accidents or surprises occur. He calls the shots.

2. We take Him at His Word. We believe His promises (the Bible is full of them—by the hundreds).

3. We claim them by faith. We apply them to our particular circumstance almost as if God were speaking directly to us this very moment.

4. We rest in Him. We consciously refuse to worry or fret over how He is going to work things out. By entering into that rest, we cease from our own works just as deliberately as our Creator-God ceased from His works on the seventh day of the creative week.

5. We continue in that calm frame of mind until God sovereignly intervenes and solves the problem. We keep trusting in Him with all our hearts. And every time an alien thought of anxiety flits through our minds, we turn it over to the Lord in prayer.

PEACE ... IN SPITE OF PANIC

Do you remember the first Apollo moon launch years ago? The astronauts, of course, were being closely monitored. At the time of lift-off, it was reported that their pulse rate was the same as just before or just after. Can you imagine? Man, if I'd have been in one of those helmets I'd have said, "Wow! Look at that! We're LEAVING! We're going! We're on our way! Look, guys, lean over here. Hey, look at this side." My heart rate would've soared! Not theirs. They probably said, "Well, it is now 10:15. Ho-hum . . . We just left. Wake up, Frank. Frank! Ralph, wake up Frank over there. He's not taking in the sights . . . (sounds of snoring)."

That's the result of great training. And, spiritually, we can be like those astronauts. That's the whole purpose of having a permanent Rock beneath us.

—*Chuck Swindoll*

YOU'RE AIMING TO . . .

■ Help group members understand God's principles of peace and determine how to incorporate them into their lives.

YOU'LL STUDY . . .

■ Acts 19:21-41; Isaiah 26:3-4
■ Major themes from Chapter 2 of the book, *Stress Fractures*

YOU'LL NEED . . .

■ Copies of Resource 2A, "Paul in the Spotlight"
■ Copies of Resource 2B, "Peace in Action"
■ Pencils
■ Chalkboard and chalk or newsprint and marker
■ Copies of Resource 3A, "When the Unexpected Strikes" (optional)
■ Bibles

Step 1 (*5 minutes*)

Panic Pictures

Turning Our Thoughts to Panic-filled Situations

I'm going to list some situations. I want you to indicate the level of panic you would feel in those situations by the following signals.

No panic: raise your hand and point your thumb down;

Minor panic: Raise your hand and turn the palm up;

Major panic: Raise your hand and spread it wide open.

Demonstrate each movement as you describe it. Then read the following items or create some of your own if you like.

• Finding that your car is out of gas and rolling into a gas station that is closed;

• Getting up to speak and discovering that you've lost your notes;

• Sitting in a sky ride gondola as it moves over an amusement park;

• Hearing that your mother-in-law is in route to your house;

• Listening to a doctor tell you that you must endure a lifetime without chocolate.

We're all panicked by different things, most of which are more serious than these items. Panic is a form of stress. Panic thrashes us around for a few minutes like a dragon would do and then leaves us too drained to adequately cope with life. Today we'll see what things could have panicked the apostle Paul and how he responded.

Step 2 (*20-25 minutes*)

Celebrity Interview

Examining Paul's Peacefulness in a Panicky Situation

Pass out copies of "Paul in the Spotlight" (Resource 2A). Ask people to choose partners.

Read Acts 19:21-41 and answer these questions as if you were the apostle Paul being interviewed. After you've finished, practice presenting the interview with one of you as Paul and the other as the interviewer.

After group members have had time to work on this, ask two or three pairs to present their interviews. Then discuss answers further. The following information may be useful to you.

1. **What was your dream at this moment in your life? How close were you to fulfilling your dream?** (To go to Rome [vss. 21, 22]; Paul delayed fulfilling his dream by staying in Asia for a while, yet this didn't seem to frustrate him.)

For those of us who are goal-oriented as Paul was, setting aside goals can be stressful. Yet Paul seemed content to delay fulfilling his goal for awhile.

Chuck Swindoll offers some background on verses 21 and 22: "Paul is

shutting down a very successful ministry [in Ephesus]. . . . he is leaving it in order to go on his way to new vistas of ministry. . . . 'I must also see Rome!' It was a burning goal in the apostle's heart. . . . Why Rome? Why is that so significant? Rome was the Oval Office of the world, the place of ultimate clout. . . . He longed to speak to Caesar about Jesus Christ."

2. **Why was Demetrius, the silversmith, so upset with you?** (As Ephesian people became Christians, they quit worshiping Diana and buying souvenirs at her shrine, which Demetrius and the other silversmiths made [vss. 23-27]).

Chuck Swindoll offers some insight into Paul's stressful predicament: "When you declare the truth you're often blamed for it even though you didn't write it. You're just declaring it. But people have no other source to turn to. They can't take a swing at God. So those who represent the Lord and His truth become the scapegoat . . . the verbal punching bag."

3. **How did you feel when the mob dragged your companions, Gaius and Aristarchus, into the theater?** (Paul wanted to help them, but the disciples wouldn't let him. He obviously didn't want Gaius and Aristarchus taking the heat for him. Yet the Scripture doesn't give the impression that Paul panicked, just that he wanted to go to them. He seemed to accept the disciples' counsel in peace [vss. 28-31]).

Chuck Swindoll offers his reflections on how he would have been panicked in this situation: "Frankly, I'd probably take the night train to Memphis! I'd get out of there, like fast. Not Paul. . . . [Paul] has peace, which allows a person to experience a degree of invincibility. When you live free of anxiety, there is an 'envelope of invincibility' in your spirit. It surrounds you, and you don't sense the intimidation of a mob."

4. **Why did the crowd finally disperse?** (An unnamed town clerk explained to them that this was a matter for Demetrius to take to the courts, and that it would be wise to stop—or Rome might accuse them of rioting [vss. 35-41])

Chuck Swindoll explains why the clerk probably acted as he did: "He gets his paycheck from Rome . . . and Rome hates riots. He also realizes this city would soon lose its freedom if order didn't return. . . . So he knows he has to calm them down if only to keep himself on the payroll. . . . The beautiful part is that he doesn't know Paul and Paul doesn't know him, yet God uses him to quiet the multitude."

Note that you'll be using the lower portion for the end of the session. If session time is limited, you may omit some of the questions, particularly number 4.

Step 3 *(10-15 minutes)*

Peace in the Active and Passive
Examining Principles of Peace

Hand out "Peace in Action" (Resource 2B) to group members who didn't receive it last week—or who haven't brought their copies. Give them a minute to read definition 1 and the explanation.

Then discuss: **Paul showed this kind of peace by serving faithfully in Asia**

Minor even though his dream was to go on to Rome. **What dreams, especially parts of the "American dream," do we get frustrated over when they aren't fulfilled?** (We want it all: meaningful careers, happy marriages, well-adjusted children, stable and even mushrooming finances. And we want them now. We don't want to take years to work on marriages or find the right "career path.")

Have people read the rest of the sheet. Then discuss: **Paul showed this kind of peace by following the advice of friends and not "rescuing" his companions from the mob. What unpleasant circumstances rattle us to the point of wanting to "fix" them or rescue someone?** (When family members experience physical or emotional difficulties; when shakeups in world affairs or work settings make us feel chaotic.)

Paul showed this kind of peace by the way he waited for God, who provided a civil servant of Rome to disband the mob. What kinds of uncertain situations make most of us feel panicky? (Situations in which we aren't in control.)

Peace is often referred to as "active waiting." The first principle on the sheet is the only one that tells us to do something; that is to remain faithful, to do what we already know is right. The second addresses our emotions—to stay calm. The third describes an attitude—to wait patiently, which in itself is saying that we are not to do anything, but to wait.

Ask group members to read the principles again carefully and write a "1" next to the principle that is most difficult for them; a "2" next to the one that is the next most difficult; and a "3" by the one that is least difficult.

Step 4 *(10-15 minutes)*

Problems for the Peaceful
Applying Principles of Peace to Everyday Problems

These principles are easy to talk about, but difficult to apply. To see how they apply, let's look at two situations. With your partners, act out each of these situations twice. The first time each person will be filled with panic.

The second time, person B will do his or her best to reassure person A. Person B can use the "Peace in Action" principles.

Depending on the time you have, read one or both of the following situations and give partners time to act them out.

1. A Pain in the Back

You (person A) helped your friend (person B) move to another apartment. Now you can't stand up straight. You go from doctor to chiropractor to surgeon but nothing helps. Talk together about it.

2. The Troubled Teens

You (person A) and your friend (person B) have teenagers who have begun coming in late and talking back even more than usual.

After the "peace-filled" roleplay about back pain, discuss: **In your role play, what did (person B) do to promote peace instead of panic?**

Listen to answers. Then ask: **Did (person B) happen to use any of the "Peace**

in Action" principles from Chuck Swindoll?

They might have been used in the following ways:

1. Do as many of your normal activities as you can, but give your body the rest it needs.

2. Follow professional advice and don't allow quick-fix solutions to entice you.

3. Believe that God's timing is perfect even though you are in pain and inconvenienced.

If you have time, do the same with the "troubled teens" roleplay. "Peace in Action" principles might apply in these ways:

1. Do your best as a parent: refrain from provoking children; teach them; expect proper behavior; let them know they're loved.

2. Don't expect the worst to happen, but be ready to investigate available resources if it should happen.

3. Give the child's body, conscience, and abilities the time they need to develop.

Step 5 *5-7 minutes)*

On Our Faces
Exploring Our Own Trust for God

Overcoming the tendency to become stressed-out in panicky situations is rooted in trust for God. When we trust in the fullest sense, we have peace.

Refer group members to the verse on the lower portion of "Paul in the Spotlight" (Resource 2A). **The word "trust" here means "to throw oneself down upon one's face." Read the verse again and think of one way in which trusting God could help you have peace in spite of panic.**

Close in prayer, thanking God for the trust that group members now have in Him and asking Him to increase its potential.

Optional: Before group members leave, pass out copies of "When the Unexpected Strikes" (Resource 3A). Encourage them to read the sheet in preparation for the next session.

PAUL IN THE SPOTLIGHT

1. What was your dream at this moment in your life? How close were you to fulfilling your dream? (Acts 19:21-22)

2. Why was Demetrius, the silversmith, so upset with you? (vss. 23-27)

3. How did you feel when the mob dragged your companions, Gaius and Aristarchus, into the theater? (vss. 28-31)

4. Why did the crowd finally disperse? (vss. 35-41)

* * * * * * *

"The steadfast of mind Thou wilt keep in perfect peace, because he trusts in Thee. Trust in the LORD forever, for in God, the LORD, we have an everlasting Rock" (Isaiah 26:3, 4, NASB).

PEACE IN ACTION

1. PEACE is the ability to remain faithful in spite of the panic of unfulfilled dreams. . . .

You and I have goals and dreams and desires that are not yet fulfilled. Our tendency is to mount our racehorse and gallop in that direction, leaving the present assignments as we get on with those much more exciting dreams. Peace is the ability to remain faithful—even when those dreams are not being fulfilled. If you forget that, You'll be frustrated and your peace will quickly disappear. . . .

2. PEACE is the ability to stay calm in spite of the panic of unpleasant circumstances. . . .

If you live intimidated by people [or situations], then you need to come to terms with your lack of peace. God is bigger than any person. Learn to focus on people through the lens of God's eye, and you'll never see anyone even near His match. No mob is out of His control. You can handle it. As a child of God, greater is He who is in you than all of those people who are in the world. . . .

3. PEACE is the ability to wait patiently in spite of panic brought on by uncertainty. . . .

While you and I are panicked, not knowing about our tomorrow, God is moving clerks [see Acts 19:35-41] around His board like pawns. You and I can't see His chessboard. We don't know the right moves, because we're not God. All we know is our little square, if that! And we cannot move. "It's tough being a rook held in place by a bishop, ya know." We're afraid we'll get picked off. But there is peace as long as God has some pawns.

—*Chuck Swindoll*

WHEN YOUR COMFORT ZONE GETS THE SQUEEZE

Sometimes we suffer stress fractures because of pain and suffering that have unexpectedly broken through the front door of our lives.

Physician Scott Peck calls [pain] "the road less traveled."

Scholar C.S. Lewis refers to it as "God's megaphone."

Contemporary author Philip Yancey says it is "the gift nobody wants."

English poet Byron referred to it as "the path to truth."

. . . It's in pain that God speaks to us through His megaphone. Suffering is "the road less traveled." Affliction is "the path to truth." Hardship and adversity—these are the gifts nobody wants. Just the presence of these things in our lives creates tension. . . . [This] is the tension between acceptance and resistance. The conflict is actually a mental struggle between seeing God as a God of sovereign control and viewing Him as a God of gracious mercy. There are lessons to be learned that can only be learned along the road of affliction, hardship, and pain.

—Chuck Swindoll

YOU'RE AIMING TO . . .
■ Help group members understand that suffering is an essential, inevitable path to spiritual growth.

YOU'LL STUDY . . .
■ I Thessalonians 3:1-8
■ Major themes from Chapter 3 of the book, *Stress Fractures*

YOU'LL NEED . . .
■ Copies of Resource 3A, "When the Unexpected Strikes"
■ Copies of Resource 3B, "Comforting the Thessalonians"
■ Pencils
■ Chalkboard and chalk or newsprint and marker
■ Copies of Resource 4B, "The Downward Spiral of Defiance" (optional)
■ Bibles

Step 1 (8-10 minutes)

Sorrow's Source
Recalling Circumstances in Which We've Suffered

Before the session begins, write the following on the chalkboard or newsprint:
- THE PRETENDERS—you go numb
- THE REVOLTED—you become nauseous
- THE DETECTIVES—you demand answers even though no one has any
- THE REACTORS—you scream or cry
- OTHER _____ (give your category a name)

As group members arrive, pass out "When the Unexpected Strikes," (Resource 3A) to group members who didn't get them last week—or who haven't brought their copies. Have someone read the two anecdotes on the top of the page.

Then ask: **When these kinds of unexpected things happen to you, what is your first physical response?** (Point to chalkboard.)

Do you dismiss it from your mind because it's too terrible to think about? Do you echo Scarlett O'Hara, who said, "I'll think about that tomorrow"? (Point to "The Pretenders" on the chalkboard.)

Does your body react in its own way—you feel sick or shaky or faint? (Point to "The Revolted.")

Do you feel desperate for more details so that you can perhaps solve the problem? (Point to "The Detectives.")

Do you react in a strong emotional way by crying or yelling or becoming violent? (Point to "The Reactors.")

Or do you have another way of reacting? Many Americans turn to the refrigerator or light a cigarette. If this is your category, what would you call it?

Allow group members time to respond. If they are reluctant to share, you might tell into what category you would fit. Emphasize that these responses are typical responses for humans, but we do seem to respond differently. Perhaps they fit into different categories in different types of situations. When their children are concerned, they're "reactors"; when friends are involved, they're "detectives."

In this session, we're going to talk about how we react to suffering, to agonizing situations such as the ones we just read. We're going to look at ways that Christians commonly react, and how to react so that these events are less stressful.

Step 2 (15-20 minutes)

Ancient Comfort
Exploring Biblical Passages about Suffering

Have you ever gotten a letter from a friend when you were in the middle of a painful situation? Do you remember how good it felt to receive comfort from someone who loved and accepted you?

Or have you received one of those letters in which a would-be comforter didn't know what to say? How about one from a person who came on so strongly that he or she was almost preaching to you?

The Thessalonians were fortunate enough to receive an encouraging letter from Paul. Imagine yourself now as one of the Thessalonians. Paul had taught in your city for just three weeks when he had to leave suddenly because of Jewish opposition. You are only a recent convert from paganism, and now you've been left with little support; you're being persecuted by pagan family and friends.

Pass out copies of "Comforting the Thessalonians" (Resource 3B) and give these directions: **Read part of Paul's letter to you (I Thessalonians 3:1-6) and figure out into which category your responses would fit. Try to record one response per verse.**

Some group members may prefer to work in pairs. Explain the categories further:

Under "Thanks, I needed that!" include anything inspirational or anything you're glad or thankful that Paul said.

Under "That was hard to swallow," write something that you as a Thessalonian Christian know is true, but it's still not too pleasant.

Under "Things I've been doing right," note anything Paul mentions that shows you have been doing the right thing and not giving in.

After a few minutes, regain people's attention and ask them to share their answers. (Thanks, I needed that: Paul sent Timothy [vs. 2]; Paul longs to see the Thessalonians [vs. 6]. Hard to swallow: we have been destined for this [vs. 3]; Paul told the Thessalonians in advance [vs. 4]. Things I've been doing right: Thessalonians didn't give in to tempter [vs. 5]; Thessalonians think kindly of Paul [vs. 6].)

I Thessalonians 3:3: The phrase "we have been destined for this" may disturb some group members. There will be more about this in Step 4.

If you like, use these comments on I Thessalonians 3:5 from Chuck Swindoll to highlight important points about how we respond to suffering:

Since the Thessalonians were new Christians, Swindoll comments: "One of the great battles within young Christians occurs when the adversary strikes during a time of suffering. The adversary finds that weak link or that chink in the armor, and pushes his way in. That's when our comfort zone really gets the squeeze!"

Step 3 *(12-15 minutes)*

Secrets of Survival
Looking at Ways to Deal with Suffering

Direct group members' attention to the next section on Resource 3B, "Making Suffering Less Stressful."

Each of these points is mentioned in I Thessalonians 3:6-8. (Read these verses.) **As I explain each of these points, mark on the continuum line where your normal response occurs in each category.** Use the material that follows as needed.

"Think kindly" of other Christians (vs. 6)—The Thessalonians thought kindly of Paul even though they were suffering. Chuck Swindoll notes: ". . . One of the signs of a twisted response to affliction is resenting a former authority. Guess who gets the business when a Christian in a congregation defects? The defecting Christian will often come back at the teacher . . . pastor . . . the one who counseled him or her."

Find support from others—The Thessalonians were "longing to see us" [Paul and his companions] (vs. 6). Swindoll notes: "So often, when people are in a time of distress amidst afflictions, they tend to go to the other side of the street when they see someone familiar approaching. They don't want to answer their phone calls. They don't want to relate to anyone else. They want to be aloof, distant, isolated. The worst place in the world to be when going through doubts is all alone. You need a friend . . . to support you."

Remain committed to spiritual truth—Timothy brought good news of the Thessalonians' faith and love (vs. 6), and Paul and his companions were comforted in hearing about the Thessalonians' faith. As Chuck Swindoll points out, suffering seems to make some indifferent regarding former teaching. They begin to doubt what they were once taught. But the Thessalonians had a firm commitment to spiritual truth (vs. 8). Paul's words could be paraphrased this way: "We were so encouraged to know you're still believing in prayer, you're still trusting in God, you're still counting on Him to be glorified."

Why are these correct responses so difficult for us? (To "think kindly" of other Christians and to remain committed to spiritual truth are difficult because we look for someone to blame our suffering on, someone on whom to vent our anger. Sometimes we prefer to isolate ourselves so that no one knows how badly we're hurting. We prefer to wear a mask of indestructibility.)

Step 4 (12-15 minutes)

Myths that Miss
Examining Misconceptions about Suffering

Part of the problem we have with suffering is that we resent it because we misunderstand it. This misunderstanding makes pain more stressful to endure.

Direct group members' attention to the lower portion of Resource 3A, "Should Christians Suffer?" Before asking someone to read it aloud, say:

In the stories at the top of this page, Cynthia and Craig are faced with devastating news. Let's imagine for a minute that they respond by thinking: "I don't deserve this. Christians shouldn't suffer. Why doesn't God fix this?"

As we read "Should Christians Suffer?" underline any ideas that could be helpful to Cynthia and Craig as they work through their feelings of devastation.

After "Should Christians Suffer?" is read, ask people to share what they underlined. ("All suffering is rooted in the fact that sin has entered the human race" may help them not feel guilty or faithless. The third and fourth paragraphs might help them see how they're giving their full attention to God, too.)

Ask the following questions if you have time:

How does our culture seek to relieve suffering? (We have all kinds of pain relievers in our culture: prescription drugs relieve physical pain; counselors, illegal drugs, and even suicide "relieve" emotional pain; divorce "relieves" marital pain [but brings its own pain].)

Why does pain "get our attention" so well? (We can't get rid of it on our own, so we turn to God for help.)

How can a Christian be "realistically trained" about suffering? (When Paul taught the Thessalonians, he warned them about suffering to come. We should warn new Christians in the same way.)

Some people misinterpret phrases such as, "you can handle [suffering] with remarkable inner peace," to mean that we should ignore the problem and it will go away. That isn't true. What practical things can we do to find that peace during suffering?

As needed, point out that it often helps to cry out to God in prayer as David did in the Psalms [for example, Psalm 77]. Verses such as the ones in this session encourage us as well. Worshiping God reminds us of His power to overcome impossible situations. Other specific ideas will be covered in the next step.

Step 5 (*5 minutes*)

Attitude Check
Examining Ways That Suffering Has Blessed Us

A.W. Tozer, as quoted by Chuck Swindoll, wrote: "It is doubtful whether God can bless a man greatly until He has hurt him deeply." This can be hard to swallow, but it's true.

Think back to a time that you suffered—perhaps your children were in danger or you faced a severe physical problem. Did God bless you greatly? If so, how? If not, could you have experienced less stress and more blessing if you had understood suffering better? If you had found support in others? If you had stayed more committed to your faith?

Allow time for silent prayer in which group members can consider these questions. Close by asking God to help each person use moments of suffering to grow closer to Him.

Optional: Before people leave, pass out copies of "The Downward Spiral of Defiance" (Resource 4B). Encourage them to read the sheet in preparation for the next session.

WHEN THE UNEXPECTED STRIKES

Cynthia has just heard that violence has broken out at the foreign university at which her son is studying. She recalls that hostages have even been taken in this unstable country. Cynthia feels uneasy. She's not sleeping well. She mentally imagines what her son might be going through.

Craig went to his physician for an annual checkup. In a few days the doctor contacted Craig and said, "We'll need to do a biopsy." After the biopsy, the doctor faced Craig with that horrible piece of information: "You have cancer."

Should Christians Suffer?
by Chuck Swindoll

There are some today who say, "All suffering is wrong. All who suffer are out of the will of God. If you suffer, you are in sin. And since you are in sin, if you will deal correctly and sufficiently with your sin, your suffering will go away."

That is simply not the truth. Scripture does not support such teaching! To be sure, all suffering is rooted in the fact that sin has entered the human race; however, not only has it been granted that we believe in Christ, but it has also been planned that we suffer.

A man told me recently, "God never had my attention until He laid me on my back. Since then, I've been listening." This strong-willed and stubborn man was fighting back the tears as he spoke those words. And he's only been in the crucible less than two weeks.

. . . Suffering is essential, not only because it softens our spirits, making us sensitive to the voice of God, but also because it reveals our true nature. It shows us the truth about ourselves. . . . No one in God's family can remain a stranger to pain and suffering.

. . . If you have been faithfully and realistically trained, you have been equipped to handle this part of God's training program. You can stand firm through your journey along the avenue of affliction. When your comfort zone gets the squeeze, you're not blown away. You can handle it with remarkable inner peace.

COMFORTING THE THESSALONIANS

Imagine yourself in the Thessalonians' place: Paul had taught there just three weeks when he had to leave suddenly because of the opposition of the Jews. Recent converts from paganism were thus left with little support in the midst of persecution.

You have received a letter from this great preacher, Paul. Read the letter (I Thessalonians 3:1-6) and jot down your responses in the following categories:

THANKS, I NEEDED THAT!

THAT WAS HARD TO SWALLOW!

THINGS I'VE BEEN DOING RIGHT!

Making Suffering Less Stressful

When suffering comes . . .

I "think kindly" of other Christians (vs. 6)	I resent other Christians, authorities, God
I find support from others (vs. 6)	I isolate myself from others
I remain committed to spiritual truth (vs. 8)	I doubt my faith

DEALING WITH DEFIANCE

Session 4

Defiance and stress are inseparable co-conspirators. Together, they scheme to steal your peace of mind.

Although the term *defiance* does not appear in Scripture, acts and attitudes of defiance often do. No matter what the term, the scene is never pretty.

The same is true in life today . . . but the tragedy is that defiance is frequently permitted and sometimes totally ignored, leaving others in the wake of its serious consequences. Talk about stress fractures!

God never overlooks or winks at defiance. He deals with it, and we are to take our cues from our Lord.

—Chuck Swindoll

YOU'RE AIMING TO . . .
- Help group members see how God deals with defiance and to recognize it in ourselves so we can deal with it, too.

YOU'LL STUDY . . .
- I Kings 11:1-14, 23, 31; Proverbs 5:21-23
- Major themes from Chapter 4 of the book, *Stress Fractures*

YOU'LL NEED . . .
- Copies of Resource 4A, "Defiance: When Solomon's Wisdom Failed"
- Copies of Resource 4B, "The Downward Spiral of Defiance"
- Pencils
- Chalkboard and chalk or newsprint and marker
- Copies of Resource 5B, "Military Success—of a Different Kind" (optional)
- Bibles

Step 1 *(5-10 minutes)*

The Defiant Ones
Exploring How Common Defiance Is

Write the following phrases on the chalkboard or newsprint before the session so that group members will begin thinking about them as they arrive:
- Staying on a diet when someone at work brings in your favorite kind of dough-nuts;
- Being nice to a neighbor who doesn't take care of his yard and lets his dog wreck your yard;
- Not giving in to a crabby mood;
- Spending every penny of a tax refund wisely;
- Not crossing the railroad tracks at the last minute even though the oncoming train is slow;
- Being told what to do by (pick at least one): your mother, a security guard at the mall, a fellow church member, or someone younger than you.

As the session begins, say: **Most of us may want to do what is right. But occasionally part of us grits our teeth and says, "I know I should do this, but I don't want to do it. Today is an exception to the rules. I'm going to let go and do what I want." On the board are written some situations in which we think those thoughts.**

Ask the group to help you list at least five more situations.

In this session, we're going to talk about one cause of stress—defiance. When we first begin to feel defiant, it may not seem stressful at all. It may even feel good to rebel. But as defiance grows, the consequences grow until plenty of stress is created.

Step 2 *(20-25 minutes)*

Even "Good Guys" Get Defiant
Examining Solomon's Defiance and Its Consequences

Form small groups. Pass out copies of Resource 4A, "Defiance: When Solomon's Wisdom Failed."

We usually think of King Solomon of Israel as the wisest man who ever lived, and as the writer of wise sayings in Proverbs. Yet he defied God's laws for Israel and brought stress on himself and his whole kingdom. This handout shows Solomon's decline after he defied God's laws. Read I Kings 11:1-14 and fill in the verse or verses that correspond with each of the events in Solomon's life.

After allowing groups time to work, ask a group to volunteer its answer for compromise and use the following information as needed for discussion. Do the same with the other points on the sheet.

Compromise (vss. 1, 2)—Even though Solomon's Hebrew upbringing included strong admonitions against intermarrying with Gentiles, he married many foreign women. He didn't marry just one; he committed adultery by marrying many of them. Swindoll comments on the defiant way in which "Solomon held fast to these in love" (vs. 2): "He not only embraced them [his foreign wives], he embraced them publicly. He not only married them, he courted them in front of the people of Israel."

Turned off to spiritual things—Solomon's wives turned his heart away (vs. 3) so that he was not wholly devoted to God (vs. 4).

Idolatry—Solomon worshiped the pagan gods of his wives (vss. 5, 6).

God warns Solomon—God appeared twice to Solomon, warning him not to go after other gods (vs. 9).

God promises to tear the kingdom from him—In verse 11, God made this promise. (In verse 31, God told Jeroboam, Solomon's friend and confidant, that He would give him ten tribes of Israel.) Chuck Swindoll compares this scolding to his experience as a disobedient child: "It's like what my folks used to say when I finally went too far. In a tone clearly reserved for finality, they would say, 'Charles, THAT'S IT!' Oh—those awful two words! . . . At times God says to His children, 'That's it! No more!' And He moves right in. Defiance, . . . more often than any other attitude, is the thing that kindles God's anger."

God raises up adversaries (vs. 14)—God raised up Hadad the Edomite against Solomon. (Verse 23 says that God raised another enemy against Solomon, Rezon, a marauder turned ruler. So God raised up these two adversaries as well as Jeroboam.)

Chuck Swindoll talks about how God raises up adversaries today as well: "When we have the audacity to defy the living God, . . . He has ways of calling all kinds of dogs from any number of alleys. . . . Sometimes they come in the form of a memory . . . it haunts you, it won't leave you alone. . . . It's like a monkey on your back—it stays, plagues, works, harasses, beats you black and blue emotionally. Perhaps your sense of defiance gets stronger, and you stiffen your neck and stand your ground. Guess what? God just calls more of those dogs out of the alley."

Step 3 (20-25 minutes)

Dabbling in Defiance
Seeing How Defiance Plays Itself Out in Our Lives

Pass out copies of Resource 4B, "The Downward Spiral of Defiance," to group members who didn't get them last time—or who haven't brought their copies. Give them time to read it silently while you write the following words on the chalkboard or newsprint.

• CARNAL ATTITUDES (selfishness, stubbornness, indifference, resistance, contempt)

• PERSONAL MISERY

• INESCAPABLE BONDAGE

(If you'd like, write the terms on a downward spiral diagram.)

Notice these three steps in defiance and the attitudes that form the first step. Let's look at how this spiral works.

Read (or have a volunteer read) the following story. Point to each step on the chalkboard as it appears in parentheses.

Steve never had much money so when he started his dry cleaning business he wanted to make as large a profit as he could. He was fun to work for, but he paid his few employees as little as possible (selfishness).

A few of his employees worked hard and proved that they were trustworthy, so Steve trained them to do the bookkeeping and manage the store. They set the tone so that all the employees worked hard. When they asked for suitable raises, he refused and gave them minimal ones (stubbornness).

These employees, with whom Steve had gotten along well before, were now disappointed in him. It showed in their attitudes. He decided not to let it bother him even though he missed the fun they used to have (indifference).

They asked Steve for another raise and he refused. When they gave him notice that they were quitting, Steve still did not budge from his position (resistance).

Steve found other employees instead who didn't work so hard and who didn't demand as much. He knew they weren't as diligent and he put them down behind their backs (contempt).

Steve found that he had to be at the dry cleaning store all the time after that because these new workers goofed off so much. Steve had no time for himself or his family and became negative about life (personal misery).

His employees, in turn, despised him and stole from him. They ruined clothing and pretended that the dry cleaning machines had malfunctioned. Steve fired a few of them, but the cycle of hiring and firing continued (inescapable bondage) so that he became a griping, intolerable friend, spouse, and father.

Steve's problems began because he violated the biblical principle that the laborer is worthy of his wages (I Timothy 5:18). Steve knew what was right, but he didn't change his ways. I'll give you the first part of another scenario and I want you to help me continue the story so that the person moves through the downward spiral of defiance much as Steve did.

Pick one of the following story leads.

• Dave and Kerrie agreed to delay starting a family so they could save for five years to buy a house. Five years have passed, but Dave insists they need to save longer so they can afford to buy in a better neighborhood. Cindy reminds him of their agreement, but he refuses to look at affordable homes. Dave has the selfish and stubborn attitudes already. He's violating Proverbs 12:22, "Lying lips are an abomination to the LORD, but those who deal faithfully are His delight." Where does the story go from here?

• Teresa sees herself as a Supermom who does it all. She is run down and keeps catching every illness that comes along. She refuses to slow down. Teresa is being selfish and stubborn in her self-sufficiency. She refuses to take care of herself and is violating I Corinthians 6:19: "Your body is a temple of the Holy Spirit . . ." Where does the story go from here?

• Mark is tired of the way his neighbor neglects his yard, so Mark has quit talking to him. When the neighbor asks to borrow a lawn tool, Mark says his is broken. Mark's selfishness has blossomed into stubbornness. He is violating Ephesians 4:32: "Be kind to one another . . ." Where does the story go from here?

After you work together to finish the story, point out the stress that this person's defiance created. Note how the main character could have avoided these problems by not rebelling against Scripture. (Dave could have honored his agreement. Teresa could have take care of her body. Mark could have tried to be kind to his neighbor.)

Step 4 *(3-5 minutes)*

Degrees of Defiance
Pinpointing Our Defiant Ways

Introduce this conclusion with Chuck Swindoll's insightful comments: **"I'm much more concerned about 'acceptable' defiance than bold defiance. Why? Because that's what happens more often than not. We cover up. We hide our defiance. We sit on the lid. But, sure enough—given sufficient pressure— something eventually snaps.**

"Your defiance will come out in the most amazing ways: a battered child; a crime of passion; a blistering tongue-lashing; running away from home; an illicit pregnancy; an ugly, caustic line of profane words; an affair; domestic disharmony; a ruined testimony. . . . Deal severely with this giant. It may be slumbering right now—but . . . not for long."

Write the following incomplete sentences on the chalkboard:
• The area in my life in which I'm most clearly defiant is:
• My defiance is bound to bring on me the consequences of:

Ask group members to use the blank side of one of their Resource sheets to complete both of these sentences. After allowing them time to do so, close in prayer, asking God for determination to overcome defiance.

Optional: Before group members leave, pass out copies of "Military Success—of a Different Kind" (Resource 5B). Encourage them to read the sheet in preparation for the next session.

DEFIANCE: WHEN SOLOMON'S WISDOM FAILED

I Kings 11:1-14

SPIRITUAL HEALTH

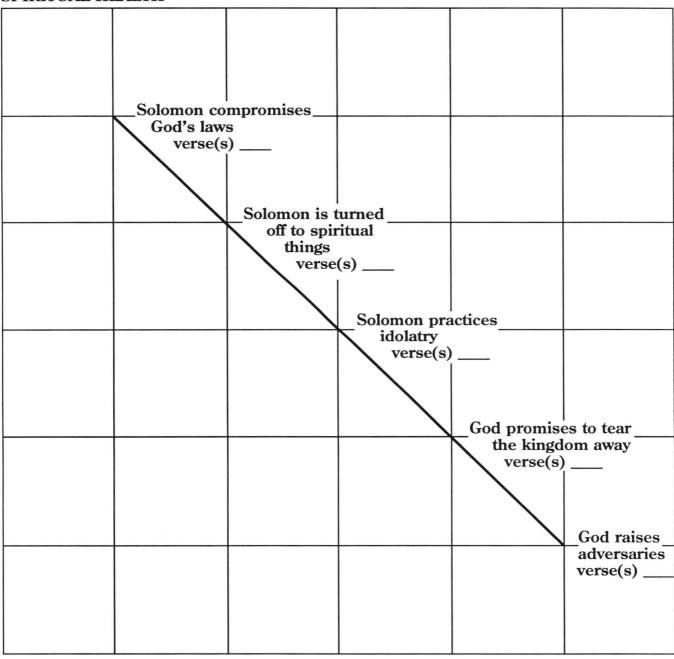

Solomon compromises
God's laws
verse(s) ____

Solomon is turned
off to spiritual
things
verse(s) ____

Solomon practices
idolatry
verse(s) ____

God promises to tear
the kingdom away
verse(s) ____

God raises
adversaries
verse(s) ____

SPIRITUAL RUIN

THE DOWNWARD SPIRAL OF DEFIANCE

STEP 1: CARNAL ATTITUDES

Long before there are carnal actions, there are carnal attitudes. It can happen to adults just as quickly as it can to teens or kids. Perhaps it would help if I spelled out a few of the attitudes by describing some actual thoughts in the minds of the defiant.

The first thought says: "I want my own way." Those who are defiant aren't interested in your way, or God's way. "I want my way." That is an attitude of selfishness.

The second thought says this: "I won't quit until I get it." That is an attitude of stubbornness. "I want my way, and I want it when I want it. I will not quit until I get it." That's just plain obstinance; that's stubbornness.

Third: "I don't care who it hurts." In other words, "I want my way. I won't quit until I get it, and I don't care who it hurts—husband, wife, peers, parents, kids, the team, my church—I don't care. I'm gonna get my way." That is an attitude of indifference.

Fourth: "I refuse to listen to counsel." Obviously, that is an attitude of resistance. "I know God has something to tell me, but I don't want to hear what He's got to say." Or, "I know what He's going to tell me—I know what that Book says. I don't want to listen to God's counsel." That's resistance.

Fifth, and finally: "I am not concerned about the consequences." That's contempt. Pushed to the wall, this extreme reaction includes ignoring the consequences—a total lack of concern for the results.

STEP 2: PERSONAL MISERY

Remember Hadad, Rezon, and Jeroboam? They dealt Solomon untold misery. The defiant person wants freedom, but he finds himself captured. He wants his own way, but he finds himself ensnared by the restrictions that misery brings.

STEP 3: INESCAPABLE BONDAGE

"For the ways of a man are before the eyes of the LORD, and He watches all his paths. His own iniquities will capture the wicked, and he will be held with the cords of his sin. He will die for lack of instruction, and in the greatness of his folly he will go astray" [Proverbs 5:21-23].

—Chuck Swindoll

MORAL PURITY

Session 5

Many of us find ourselves stressed to the breaking point as we endure a two-sided battle: On one front, we must cope with a rapidly declining culture—a society racing into a foundationless moral chaos. On a deeply personal level, we find ourselves wrestling daily with a menacing, unrelenting adversary called "Lust." . . .

Our minds and our emotions are easily lured off target by . . . "the system," . . . the endless, relentless bombardment from the world in which we live. Its messages are subtle and bold, written and spoken, always attractive, remarkably convincing, and clever indeed. . . .

Erroneous thinking that leads to evil actions needs to be confronted. Because "the system" operates twenty-four hours a day, seven days every week, it's doubtful that Christians have come anywhere near overstating their position. With determination and diligence, we must continue to make known a perspective that exposes "the system" and penetrates the moral fog which envelops all who live on this planet.

—Chuck Swindoll

YOU'RE AIMING TO . . .
■ Help group members understand what it means to be unblamable (or blameless) in the area of moral purity and inspire them to incorporate that into their lives.

YOU'LL STUDY . . .
■ I Thessalonians 3:11-13, 4:1-8
■ Major themes from Chapter 5 of the book, *Stress Fractures*

YOU'LL NEED . . .
■ Copies of Resource 5A, "How Well Do You Know Yourself?"
■ Copies of Resource 5B, "Military Success—of a Different Kind"
■ Pencils
■ Chalkboard and chalk or newsprint and markers
■ Copies of Resource 6A, "The Price Tags for Purity" (optional)
■ Bibles

Step 1 *(5-7 minutes)*

Self-Study
Seeing If We're Good "Students" of Ourselves

Pass out copies of "How Well Do You Know Yourself?" (Resource 5A). Ask group members to mark their answers to the three multiple-choice questions.

After they're finished, say: **Trade papers with someone who knows you and let him or her evaluate your answers. Did they accurately reflect what the person knows you're like? The person should place a check mark by the ones with which he or she agrees.**

Then have people give back their papers and look at how they scored.

Moral purity is one area in which it is important to be "a student of yourself." In the next two sessions, we're going to talk about how to avoid the stress that comes from moral pollution. We'll look at what it means to be a student of yourself so that you can keep a pure, stress-free conscience.

Step 2 *(15-20 minutes)*

Command Search
Examining God's Simple but Difficult Command to Abstain

Imagine that you've been asked to teach a course entitled "Love and Sex" to the teenagers at our church. You can stop sweating—it's only hypothetical! What commands do you find in this passage that you'd want to include because they're connected to moral purity?

Ask someone to read I Thessalonians 3:11—4:8. Ask volunteers to suggest commands from the Scripture. The following are possible group responses and comments and questions you may wish to use.

"Establish your hearts unblamable in holiness" (3:13)—"Unblamable" (or blameless in some translations) means that we don't have an ounce of guilt on our conscience. We haven't led anyone on or tempted anyone.

How is being blameless different from being self-righteous? (Being self-righteous means that we see God's righteousness in ourselves and we pride ourselves in it. Being blameless means that we manage, with God's help, to avoid small temptations as well as larger ones.)

Why does it help us to be blameless? How does it keep us from feeling stressed? Chuck Swindoll describes what it means to be "unblamable": "Confident living is directly linked to being 'unblamable.' It's better than knowing the answers to all the questions on a test, or having plenty of money, or earning an advanced degree. There's no security like being free of blame."

"Abstain from sexual immorality" (4:3)—Swindoll defines "abstain" as meaning "having nothing to do" with something: "[It] doesn't simply mean 'watch out' or 'be discreet' or to indulge in 'safe sex.'"

What are some ways that people bend the rule to abstain from sexual immorality? (We make exceptions such as, "But if I really love someone, it's okay," or, "If I'm planning to marry this person, it's okay to have sex," or "I'm just flirting innocently. I'm not doing any harm.")

How could you hurt someone else with a seemingly innocent flirtation? ("Innocent" flirtation assumes that all persons present have their sexual desires under control. This is an unwise assumption, because most people battle sexual temptation privately so that others don't realize they're struggling. It can cause both married and unmarried persons alike to drift into promiscuous thoughts.)

"Know how to possess his own vessel in sanctification and honor, not in lustful passion" (4:4, 5)—Swindoll advises, ". . . You must become a student of yourself in order to know how to handle your battle with sexual lust. Those who fail to know themselves will lose the battle and ultimately become enslaved to lust. . . . there must be a practical, working knowledge of one's own tendencies."

"No man transgress and defraud his brother in this matter" (vs. 6)—Apparently, some persons actually excused sexual immorality if it was between family members (incest) or fellow Christians. This, of course, is also wrong.

Thank group members for their participation. **At different times in our lives, most of us find these commands difficult to obey. Chuck Swindoll shares with us how he dealt with these struggles at a difficult time in his life.**

Step 3 (10-12 minutes)

A Success Story
Examining How Chuck Swindoll Battled Sexual Temptation

Pass out copies of "Military Success—of a Different Kind" (Resource 5B) to group members who didn't get them last time—or who haven't brought their copies. Let people read the sheet aloud or silently.

Why do you think Chuck Swindoll was successful in remaining faithful to his wife? (He called on God for help and received it. He avoided temptation by not going into the village. He planned ahead; when he got off the bus, he went straight to his destination. He filled his life with music and sports—both things he enjoyed.)

Have you ever faced tough sexual temptation and won? (You may want to have a story of your own ready in case no one opens up. If someone does, notice the type of situation he or she was in and ask whether or not that occurs frequently today.)

Perhaps you haven't been as "successful" as Chuck Swindoll was in the service. You may think that because you've failed in the past that you can never walk in purity. But you can start over. God can supply you with the power to change and begin again.

Innocent and Not Proven Otherwise

Examining What We Can Do to Be Blameless

How do you think Chuck Swindoll's moral victory in the military helped him in later years?
Swindoll describes how this helped him feel blameless: "Had I not been preserved from unfaithfulness, I would have to pass rather hurriedly and embarrassingly over this passage and similar sections of Scripture. I sincerely doubt that I would have pursued the ministry had I fallen into sexual lust."

Can we become overconfident in facing temptation? (Christians especially can think they're invincible because they know God and spend time in His Word.) Swindoll provides an honest model of what temptation is like for a Christian: ". . . Temptation is so fierce I have to be almost rude to the opposite sex. That may not sound very nice, but that's the price I'm willing to pay. It is worth it."

Chuck Swindoll is not alone in his fight to remain morally pure, of course. When asked how he built moral safeguards into his life, Billy Graham said that he had been tempted, but that he took precautions of never having a meal alone with a woman other than [his wife] Ruth, not even in a restaurant. He never rode in an automobile alone with a woman. ("William Franklin Graham: Seventy Exceptional Years," *Christianity Today,* November 18, 1988.)

Should we adopt the rules that Swindoll and Graham set for themselves? (We could become legalistic in following all their guidelines and might try to impose them on others, too. The important thing is that they were "students of themselves." They knew what could trip them up and they avoided it. We should follow their example.)

How do we set our own guidelines? (As we become good students of ourselves, we learn what situations are most difficult for us and we avoid these. Hearing what Graham or Swindoll did can give us ideas and help us figure out our own guidelines.)

What guidelines could the following people set for themselves? (Besides the ones suggested, Scripture reading and prayer are applicable in all these situations.)

• **Diane, who is single, wants to go back to her high school reunion. But an old boyfriend has just called to see if she'll be there. She was not a Christian at the time, and they were involved sexually.** (If Diane has a girlfriend she can confide in and who is attending the reunion, they can stick together. [It would be good if this friend is a Christian, too.] Or Diane could ask a male Christian friend to go as an escort. She might attend only a small portion of the reunion.)

• **Paul notices that he is especially attracted to his co-worker on days when she wears a certain outfit.** (Paul could discipline himself to avoid looking at her on those days; if he thought she would understand, he could ask her not to wear the outfit; he could learn to mentally associate the outfit with an anti-temptation Bible verse he's memorized, or use the outfit as a visual reminder to pray for strength to resist temptation.)

• **Candy, who is married, feels attracted to her pastor.** (She can avoid all situations in which she might be alone with him. If theirs is a "hugging" church, she can avoid that, too. She may even need to avoid shaking hands with him at the front door. If the attraction is out of control, she may need to change churches or work in a ministry outside the worship service for a while.)

• **Steve, who is married, is fantasizing about a woman in the choir.** (Steve can confess this to a mature Christian friend and become accountable to him to stop. This guideline could work for the other examples as well.)

Step 5 *(5-7 minutes)*

Becoming "Students of Ourselves"
Exploring the Ways We Fall into Temptation

Each of us is tempted by different sources. Some of these may seem silly to others. Says Chuck Swindoll: "There are certain people who, by their suggestive conversation, weaken us. There are settings too tempting, touches too personal, and liberties that are too much for us to handle. We are fools to play around with them. They create appeal in temptations we simply cannot control. So, if we are committed to abstain, we stay clear of them."

Refocus group members' attention on "How Well Do You Know Yourself?" (Resource 5A). Explain: **The lower portion pictures the path to blamelessness that God wants all of us to follow. Write by the "side roads" the situations that get you sidetracked morally. Be as honest as you can; use initials or code words if you don't want to write anything embarrassing. Some of the questions at the bottom may help you.**

Close in prayer, allowing a silent time for people to look again at their "side roads" and commit themselves to avoiding those situations.

Optional: Before group members leave, pass out copies of "The Price Tags for Purity" (Resource 6A). Encourage them to read the sheet in preparation for the next session.

HOW WELL DO YOU KNOW YOURSELF?

If people get mad at me, I usually:
a) get mad, too;
b) try to calm them down;
c) wonder what they ate for breakfast;
d) other.

If I don't understand a joke, I:
a) laugh anyway;
b) ask the person to explain it;
c) quickly move on to someone else who isn't so clever;
d) other.

If I forget to take something with me to work or on a trip, I:
a) buy another one;
b) do nothing except complain about it endlessly;
c) make do with something else, which usually turns out to work better anyway;
d) other.

3 checks = You are truly a "student of yourself."
2 checks = You may be a "student of the person you'd like to be."
1 checks = You may be a student of someone other than yourself.
0 checks = Ask the person who graded your paper to introduce you to yourself.

What kinds of music, magazines, films, or television programs make me most vulnerable to temptation?

Is there another person, perhaps a same-sex friend, who gets me talking and thinking about things that make me vulnerable?

Do certain kinds of parties or pastimes bother me?

MILITARY SUCCESS — OF A DIFFERENT KIND

by Chuck Swindoll

My wife and I were married in June of 1955. We both were quite young. I finished my schooling and then faced the need to fulfill my military obligation. . . .

Before I ever dropped the sea bag off my shoulder on the island of Okinawa, I was faced with a tough decision. I was going to make my home in barracks characterized by a godless lifestyle. Venereal disease was not uncommon among those on the island. Living with a woman in the village was as common as breathing smog in southern California. If you lived in Okinawa, you slept around. . . .

I realized, especially since I had known the joys of intimacy in marriage, that temptation would be incredibly strong. . . . Candidly, I had to be tough on myself. There were times when I had to be downright brutal with my emotions. I had to make some tough, Spartan decisions . . . unpopular decisions among a bunch of guys who tried everything in the book to tempt me. . . .

Let me clarify something, lest you misunderstand. God showed me it wasn't my job to clean up the goldfish bowl; it was my job to fish. I wasn't called to lead a flagwaving crusade for moral purity across the Orient. It was my job to live clean whether anybody else did or not. To put it bluntly, I was not to put my hands on someone who wasn't my wife. I wasn't even to talk about such things. . . .

God made it clear to me that if I would abstain from sexual immorality, He would honor that. His Spirit came to my rescue time and again. I had no corner on strength. I was often in the path of temptation, as anyone reading these words right now would understand, but I refused to surrender. Those were lonely days away from home for almost eighteen months. I was often burning with desire for my wife. But, thank God, I was committed to abstaining from immorality.

How did I make it? I involved myself in things that were wholesome, things that paid off, things that kept me busy, active and fulfilled. I cultivated my musical abilities by becoming much more proficient in several instruments. I was also involved in an aggressive athletic program, spending most of my spare time with men who were committed to the same wholesome objectives. In my mind, the village was "off limits." I didn't even drop in and get a soft drink in the village bars. I couldn't handle it. When I got off the bus that took me to my destination, I looked straight ahead and walked fast. That little island had physically attractive women and over five thousand places of prostitution. I never touched one of them. Obviously I saw them . . . but I refused to yield.

RESISTING THE LURE OF LUST

Session 6

Red-blooded, healthy American men and women struggle with the same savage—lust. Non-Christians and Christians alike grapple with its presence and its persistence throughout their lives. Some think that getting married will cause temptation to flee. It doesn't. Others have tried isolation. But sensual imagination goes with them, fighting and clawing for attention and gratification.

. . . Lust is committed to wage war against your soul—in a life-and-death struggle—in hand-to-hand combat. Don't stand before this mortal enemy and argue or fight in your own strength—run for cover. . . . Lust is one flame you dare not fan. You'll get burned if you do.

. . . Our enemy, crafty and clever and experienced as he is, knows which lure best attracts each one of us. Our unique inner "itch" longs to be satisfied by that particular outer "scratch." And unless we draw upon the all-conquering power of Christ, unless we consciously apply the same biblical techniques Joseph applied, we'll yield. We'll bite the bait, and we'll suffer the horrible [and stressful] consequences.

—*Chuck Swindoll*

YOU'RE AIMING TO . . .
- Help group members understand necessary attitudes and methods to avoid giving in to lust.

YOU'LL STUDY . . .
- Genesis 39:1-23; Matthew 4:1-11; I Corinthians 6:18-20; 10:13; Ephesians 6:10-17; Matthew 5:28; James 1:14-16
- Major themes from Chapter 6 of the book, *Stress Fractures*

YOU'LL NEED . . .
- Copies of Resource 6A, "The Price Tags for Purity"
- Copies of Resource 6B, "Putting Words in Their Mouths"
- Pencils and paper
- Chalkboard and chalk or newsprint and markers
- Copies of Resource 7B, "A Challenge to Men, a Prayer for Women" (optional)
- Bibles

59

Step 1 *(5-7 minutes)*

Weird Stories
Introducing the Stresses Involved in Lust

Ask your group to call out specific examples of each of the following three items. Then pick one in each category and write it in the appropriate blank below. (Don't let people know in advance how you're going to use the words. Pick the most unusual suggestions so that the sentences turn out to be as absurd as possible.)

(1) a tall object
(2) a gooey substance
(3) a heavy object

Now read the resulting sentences to the group.

Bart spends so much time staring at women on the street that he has run his car into a (1) _____ seven times.

Sandy and her friends are gaining weight because they get together to eat (2) _____ pie and talk about how their husbands should be more like their romance novel hero, Baron Barry DeBiceps.

The last time Marsha's boss made a pass at her, she picked up the (3) _____ sitting on her desk and hurled it at him.

After having fun with the absurdity of the sentences, continue:

These are silly sentences, but the issues they bring up are serious. The characters in these sentences are stressed because of how they're responding to their own lust or someone else's.

In this session, we'll get more specific about the subject of last session's discussion—moral purity. We'll see how another person's lust caused stress in Joseph's life; he moved from being a respected overseer to a prisoner. We'll explore ways to control our lust, which will, in turn, help us avoid further stress.

Step 2 *(20-25 minutes)*

What If I Were Joseph?
Examining Joseph's Behavior in Tempting Circumstances

As we take turns reading Genesis 39:1-23 aloud, think about how Joseph might have felt as these events progressed.

After the reading, form small groups. Distribute paper and pencils to each group. Assign each group one of these sets of verses from Genesis 39: vss. 1-6, 7-10, 11-16, and 17-23.

As a small group, write a journal entry that Joseph could have written during the events in your Scripture passage. Record how you think Joseph could have been feeling about life, about God, or about Potiphar's wife.

Distribute "The Price Tags for Purity," Resource 6A, to group members who didn't get them last week—or who haven't brought their copies. **Look at the sections on "The Price Tags for Purity" that correlate with your assigned verses for additional insights.**

After allowing groups time to work, regain their attention and ask them to share their entries. After each group shares, discuss its insights using the following information.

Vss. 1-6—Even though Joseph was a slave, it probably felt good to be so trusted and respected. He was handsome, and it may have been flattering that the boss's wife was attracted to him.

Yet "the good life" can be difficult too. Chuck Swindoll illustrates this with what happened to Olympic hockey hero Jim Craig as he became admired:

"His name became a household word in the homes of sports fans around the world. Offers and opportunities were an almost-everyday occurrence. The temptations were also frequent. . . . the *New York Times* [reported]: 'There was the time in Chicago when he unlocked his hotel room to find a nude woman lying on his bed (Craig said, "Please leave.") . . . There was the time in Atlanta when a girl who said she had been speaking to God about him kissed him passionately . . . and then passed out.'"

Vss. 7-10—Joseph could have used the excuses listed in section 2 of "The Price Tags for Purity," but he didn't.

What reasons did Joseph give Potiphar's wife for rejecting her? (Joseph remained loyal to Potiphar, his employer, and to God's ways. It's interesting that he never said that she wasn't attractive or that he wasn't attracted to her.)

Chuck Swindoll points out that Joseph's reaction was founded on two bases—reason ("How foolish to break the trust he had been building for years!" [vs. 8]); and conscience ("It was unthinkable that he could violate the name of his God by yielding to her advances" [vs. 9]).

Vss. 11-16—Joseph acted clearly and decisively. When Potiphar's wife grabbed him, he ran. We don't know how he felt, but he didn't think it over or try to talk her out of it. Perhaps his spiritual instinct told him that nothing would work except fleeing.

It's interesting that Joseph didn't wear down even though Potiphar's wife kept making advances. He didn't take it as some "sign" that they were supposed to be together.

Swindoll comments on this: "Every time the subject of sensual lust is discussed in the New Testament, there is one invariable command—RUN! . . . It is impossible to yield to temptation while running in the opposite direction."

Vss. 17-23—Joseph doesn't seem to blame anyone that he was falsely accused. He could have been confused and discouraged, but the text doesn't say that he was. It seems that he was open to God, because God was with him and extended kindness to him so that he found favor with the chief jailer.

Joseph illustrates how resisting lust actually decreases the stress in our life. It seems difficult at the time, but at least the conscience is clear. Having an affair would not have decreased Joseph's stress; he probably would have been killed for that. He's an example of how to be faithful and how purity works for the best.

How High Is the Price?
Considering Why Lust Calls for Drastic Measures

Refocus group members' attention on "The Price Tags for Purity" (Resource 6A) and read it together.

In what other situations are people weakened against temptation? (When they're in a troubled marriage or a marriage in which one partner travels or is disabled; when someone of the opposite sex is staying in their home; when they're around someone they have been close to before; when they spend a lot of time with someone of the opposite sex in a hobby or work setting.)

How does the second "must" explain why Christians become involved in sexual activity? (Christians "forget" God and act as if He turned around for a minute and isn't looking at them.)

Some have said that lust puts us into a temporary state of insanity. How does that explain the severity of some of these "musts"? ("Temporary insanity" calls for extreme measures. While it's usually good to listen to ourselves and let righteous actions flow out of a clean heart, this doesn't always work when we're feeling lustful. The emotions can sometimes be so out of control that it's better not to be around that person or to give him or her a chance to persuade you. [This may result in your being accused of not giving the other person a "fair chance to speak."] It is often better to flee first, as Joseph did, and deal with emotions in a safe environment away from the temptation.)

Methods to Deal with Our Madness
Exploring Ways to Respond to Lust

When you're faced with your own lust or someone else's, it takes a lot of energy just to decide what to do. Joseph apparently lessened this stress by planning ahead. It looks as if he had decided ahead of time that he would not give in no matter how he felt. In the same way, we can relieve our own stress in this area by thinking about what we could say and do in difficult situations.

Pass out "Putting Words in Their Mouths" (Resource 6B). Explain each entry in the "Actions" column, reading the example in the right-hand column and using the following information.

State logical reasons—Depending on our circumstances, we could replace the name of Potiphar in the example with a spouse or employer's name. It could also be someone we are loyal to or who would be hurt by our actions. Or the reason may have nothing to do with loyalty, but may simply be a reason why the action doesn't make sense (even if the emotions think it does!), such as, "I'll ruin my reputation."

Declare love and allegiance to God—Whether our sin involves others or not, it's always a sin against God. As we grow in Him, we may say, "I love God too much to disappoint Him this way."

Quote Scripture aloud—Jesus quoted Scripture when the devil tempted Him (Matthew 4:1-11). Chuck Swindoll notes: "Interestingly, only one offensive weapon is part of our armor described in Ephesians 6:10-17, 'the sword of the Spirit, which is the word of God.' The Greek term translated 'word' is the term meaning 'saying.' It has reference to something spoken [aloud]."

What are some other examples of Scripture that could be helpful to quote at this time? (Matthew 5:28; I Corinthians 6:18, 19, 20; James 1:14, 15, 16.)

Dismiss excuses—Re-read the excuses printed under "must" #2 on "The Price Tags for Purity."

Why should excuses not even be listened to? (No excuse will supersede the biblical commandment of abstinence. Since emotions become so confused, it's better not to even listen to excuses.)

Then read the first situation below the columns. Ask the group to offer specific examples of what Carolyn could say to herself. Do the same with the other situations. Ask for several examples for each.

Step 5 (*3-5 minutes*)

Future Walk
Planning How to Respond Better to Temptation

In this session and the previous one, we've looked at many tempting situations. No one is immune to temptation—not celebrities, not "everyday" Christians. When you least expect it, there it is again. Think of a tempting situation that has come up in your life that has not been easy. (Pause.)

Look over the handout, "Putting Words in Their Mouths," again and circle the action (in the top portion, on the left) that you need to use more often in fighting temptation. Perhaps you quote Scripture, but not aloud. If so, circle "aloud." If you never declare love and allegiance to God, circle that one.

Allow group members a minute or so to mark their papers. Then close in prayer, asking God's help in fighting sexual temptation.

Optional: Before people leave, pass out copies of "A Challenge to Men, a Prayer for Women" (Resource 7B). Encourage them to read the sheet in preparation for the next session.

THE PRICE TAGS FOR PURITY

by Chuck Swindoll

. . . Let me declare four "musts" based on Joseph's experience. These "musts" are to be applied if you expect to resist sensual temptations in your life.

1. You must not be weakened by your situation. [Genesis 39:1-6]

Economically, Joseph was secure, respected, trusted, and stable. Personally, he was handsome and desirable. He was also in charge of the entire house, so getting alone posed no problem. On top of all that, it wasn't his idea; the woman thought it up! And he was also unmarried.

2. You must not be deceived in the persuasion. [Genesis 39:7-10]

. . . When lust reaches fever pitch, [Dietrich Bonhoeffer wrote]: "God is quite unreal to us" and Satan fills us with "forgetfulness of God." . . . [Satan] attempts to cancel out tomorrow's consequences by emphasizing today's delights.

Joseph could have allowed himself to listen to the wrong voice. Men [and women] filled with lust do so every day:

"Her husband [or his wife] doesn't meet her [or his] needs like I can."
"Who will ever find out? We're safe."
"Look, we're going to be married soon."
"I'm so lonely. God will understand and forgive."
"Just this once—never, ever again."

3. You must not be gentle with your emotions. [Genesis 39:7-16]

Look again at Joseph's model (Genesis 39):
Verse 8: *He refused.*
Verse 9: *How then could I do this great evil . . .?*
Verse 10: *He did not listen to her to lie beside her . . . .*
Verse 12: *He left . . . and fled. . . .*
Be tough on yourself; boldly reject the bait! . . . Refuse to let your feelings dominate your mind when lust craves satisfaction.

4. You must not be confused with the immediate results. [Genesis 39:10-20]

. . . Even though [Joseph] resisted the woman's advances, she kept coming back. Instead of those advances tapering off, they intensified. Instead of being immediately rewarded for his self-control, he was falsely accused and dumped into a dungeon. Talk about confusing!

But Joseph kept his eyes fixed on the Lord. He refused to be disillusioned. How often I've seen people withstand a barrage of temptation for a while, then in a weak moment fall because of confusion! The enemy does not surrender easily. Keep standing firm, even though you feel strangely alone and forgotten by the Lord. Ultimately, He will reward every act of moral restraint.

PUTTING WORDS IN THEIR MOUTHS

Actions	Examples
State logical reasons	I would be violating the trust of Potiphar who I've promised to be faithful to.
Declare love and allegiance to God.	I can't sin against God like this.
Quote Scripture aloud.	"God is faithful, who will not allow you to be tempted beyond what you are able, but with the temptation will provide the way of escape." (I Corinthians 10:13)
Dismiss excuses	No matter how many "good" reasons I have to sin, I will not do it.

• Carolyn is attracted to a male co-worker who then asks her out to dinner even though she's married. What should Carolyn say to him?

• Tom buys pornographic magazines and hides them carefully so that no one knows he has them. What can Tom say to himself the next time he starts out for the convenience store to buy more magazines?

• Pam rents popular movies on videocassette quite often. She notices that when the movie features a certain male actor she fantasizes about him. What can Pam say to herself as she stands in the video store trying to decide which movie to rent?

STRESSFUL CHANGES FOR WOMEN AND MEN

Session 7

Among the stressful issues of the last two decades, the subject of the woman's role in society would certainly rank in the top ten.

. . . There's the "total" woman advocate saying true femininity means "full surrender to your man." But there's also the radical feminist . . . who sneer[s] at such "subservient advice," speaking more of absolute equality, female dominance, and assertiveness.

All the issues on this subject are much too volatile, extensive, and complicated to be solved in a single [session]. . . . one major message is clearly in need of being proclaimed because it is so obviously set forth in God's Word . . . : Women are people of worth and dignity.

If you are a woman who is beginning to doubt your value, finding yourself in need of encouragement and affirmation, or if you are a man who tends to relegate women, in general, to a subhuman role (and deep down inside you are honestly starting to wonder if that kind of thinking is more traditional than scriptural), then this [session] should help.

—Chuck Swindoll

YOU'RE AIMING TO . . .
- Help group members think about the stress that occurs because of the changing role of women in our culture and how to deal with that.

YOU'LL STUDY . . .
- Acts 16:11-15, 21:7-14; II Timothy 1:3-5, 3:15
- Major themes from Chapter 7 of the book, *Stress Fractures*

YOU'LL NEED . . .
- Copies of Resource 7A, "Balancing the Extremes"
- Copies of Resource 7B, "A Challenge to Men, a Prayer for Women"
- Pencils
- Chalkboard and chalk or newsprint and marker
- Copies of Resource 8B, "Genesis-Style Leisure" (optional)
- Bibles

Examining Extremes

Looking at the Confusion over Women's Roles

Pass out "Balancing the Extremes" (Resource 7A) and ask group members to look at the top section titled, "Driven toward Two Extremes." Read the two quotations listed at the top of the page.

These quotations represent two extreme points of view. Who are some "folk heroes" for each point of view represented by the quotations? These could be authors, speakers, famous TV or movie roles, even cartoon characters.

Get some suggestions. Then move on:

Look below the quotes at the reasons listed under "Why So Extreme?" These are adapted from Chuck Swindoll's *Stress Fractures*. Notice how these causes have bounced off each other. Submission was emphasized, so machismo flourished. This (and other factors) inspired a militant women's movement, which then inspired a backlash from some Christians. Circle any causes mentioned that you have supported.

In this session, we're going to talk about the stresses that occur because of the changing role of women in our culture. Much more could be said about the entire topic, but we're only going to look at how to deal with the stresses.

Balanced Bible Women

Examining the Way Women Were Treated in the New Testament Church

Refer the group to "A Balanced Woman of God Sees . . .", the lowest portion of Resource 7A, "Balancing the Extremes."

Write on the chalkboard or newsprint these three questions about the biblical women listed:

• *How did this woman (these women) achieve a balance between assertiveness and graciousness?*

• *How did men respond to this woman (these women)?*

• *Which of the three principles (adapted from Chuck Swindoll's book and listed under "A Balanced Woman of God Sees . . .") does she (or do they) best illustrate?*

Then read Acts 16:13-15 together and ask the questions on the board about Lydia. (First question: Lydia was assertive ["she prevailed upon us"] and gracious [she invited them to stay at her house]. She was also a competent thinker-businesswoman, yet still open and teachable.)

(Second question: She was obviously respected by the apostle Paul, for he and his companions stayed with her.)

(Third question: Lydia exemplifies principle #2. We don't know whether Lydia was married or not; but in either case, she seemed to depend only on God for security.)

Are there other women in the Bible that exemplify this kind of depth of spirituality, graciousness, and competence? (Dorcas abounded "with deeds of kindness and charity" and was well known in her community [Acts 9:36]. In Thessalonica, a "number of leading women" were responsive to Paul and Silas's teaching [Acts 17:12]. Paul called Aquila and his wife, Priscilla, "fellow-workers" [Romans 16:3].)

Read the other two passages, Acts 21:7-14 (Philip's prophetic daughters) and II Timothy 1:3-5, 3:15 (Eunice and Lois). After each one, ask the three questions on the board.

Acts 21:7-14—(First question: Paul, Luke, and their company stayed with Philip the evangelist [graciousness]. Philip's four virgin daughters were prophetesses [assertiveness—exercising their gift]. They also exhibited assertiveness and graciousness by the way they, along with the whole company, responded to Paul's decision to go to Jerusalem. They and the company (vs. 12) begged Paul not to go to, but finally reacted by falling silent and saying, "The will of the Lord be done!")

(Second question: They were so respected that Luke specifically mentioned them.)

(Third question: These women illustrate principle #3. Like the rest of the company, they couldn't resolve their differences with Paul, but they committed the problem to God.)

Say about principle #3: **Some Christians come off "like a fairy tale," says Chuck Swindoll, "promising you [women] that all your stress fractures will be mended, that life will suddenly start changing, that your husband will become all you need during the next seventy-two hours . . . The fact is . . . we must change before anyone else will . . . and even then there's no guarantee . . . [Philip's daughters] had difficulty convincing a strong man [Paul] to change his mind. In fact, they failed to do so. But rather than fighting and forcing, they . . . left the results with God."**

II Timothy 1:3-5, 3:15—(First question: Eunice and Lois, Timothy's mother and grandmother, had a deep faith and knew the Bible well in an age when most women didn't read and often knew little about Scripture. They managed to pass this on to Timothy even though Timothy's father and head of the household was Greek.)

(Second question: Paul obviously respected these women because he frequently mentioned Timothy's rich heritage of faith.)

(Third question: Eunice and Lois illustrate principle #1 because they paid so much attention to Scripture in what could have been a pagan household.)

All three of these principles emphasize that women—like men—are to make God the focus of their lives. God helps women in every area of their lives—family, career, service to others. Yet He—not these things—is the focus.

Step 3 (15-20 minutes)

Women's Worries
Exploring How God Can Meet Needs of Today's Women

Before the session, read the problems that follow. Choose three or four that you think are most likely to affect the women in your group. To help you choose, the topic of the problem is stated first.

It's difficult enough to figure out roles for women in this age, but when stress hits, it gets worse. I'm going to read some situations that highlight stresses women feel.

After reading each situation you've chosen, ask: **What suggestions can you make to Carla? Which principles under "A Balanced Woman of God Sees . . ." apply to Carla's situation?**

Answers may vary widely. In the last situation, ask the group to answer first as if Carla were married, and then as if she were a single mother.

How do any or all of these principles apply to Carla when . . .

Lack of safety—**She makes an emergency trip to the grocery store at 10 P.M. and remembers that her friend's purse was snatched in front of that same store late at night?** (In this tough but common dilemma, principle #2 applies as Carla feels competent to make a careful, wise decision. She can go home and ask someone else to come with her. She can park as closely as possible to the store and hide her money in her shoe. Principle #3 applies as she prays and asks God for His counsel.)

Intellectual exclusion—**She is excluded from conversations about politics because men figure she doesn't know or care about those things?** (#2 applies as Carla feels confident to join the conversation anyway. #3 applies as she relies on God for her self-esteem needs rather than on the men who exclude her.)

Hormonal changes which are common in most women, especially pregnant and postpartum women—**Hormones flood her system, making her feel depressed?** (#1 applies as she seeks relief from depression in biblical passages such as various psalms, Philippians 4:4-8, or the account of Elijah's depression [I Kings 19:9-21]. #3 is meaningful in that some bodily reactions are beyond her control.)

Society's dangerous focus on thinness and youth—**She feels fat and ugly, compared to the women on television?** (#1, especially I Samuel 16:7 ["looks on the heart"] and I Peter 3:3, 4 tell Carla to focus on the inner person, not solely on the outward person. #2 helps her understand the undue and even harmful influence our culture has in featuring an exaggerated and even dangerously thin and youthful appearance.)

Increasing necessity for two incomes, and high percentage of single moms living below poverty level, on welfare, and even homeless—**It's tough to make ends meet unless she gets a better job?** (#1 applies because in the Bible God offers promises to supply our needs [Philippians 4:19]. #2 helps her have the courage to try for a job that is meaningful and rewarding. #3 helps her trust those circumstances [unexpected bills, unfair job interviews] that are beyond her control.)

These statements may sound like easy clichés as they are printed on the page. But they aren't meant to be flip, instant fixes. They must be worked through over and over and in every kind of problem and every level of maturity.

Step 4 *(5 minutes)*

Balanced Homework
Planning Ways to Help Women Be All that God Intended

Pass out copies of "A Challenge to Men, a Prayer for Women" (Resource 7B) to group members who didn't get them last week—or who haven't brought their copies.

Ask the men in your group to look at the "Challenge to Men." **Women today are under unusual stresses. They need the men in their lives to consider their needs. Here are a list of questions you can ask the women in your life to help them along the road to becoming what God wants for them. Look over these questions and think of a time that would be good to approach some of these women with one of these questions.**

Ask the women to look at the "Prayer for Women." **Please read this prayer that almost any woman can relate to. Underline a sentence or two that you would like to continue to pray during the week.**

Optional: Before group members leave, pass out copies of "Genesis-Style Leisure" (Resource 8B). Encourage them to read the sheet in preparation for the next session.

BALANCING THE EXTREMES

Driven toward Two Extremes

"FULL SURRENDER TO YOUR MAN" PHILOSOPHY
"Women should be kept barefoot and pregnant." *(Author unknown)*

SNEERING AT SUBSERVIENT SERVICE
"I'm loud, and I'm vulgar, and I wear the pants in this house because somebody's got to . . ." (from *Who's Afraid of Virginia Woolf?*)

Why So Extreme?

1. A misunderstanding and misapplication of "submission," as spinelessness, passivity and waiting on the whim of her man.

2. A failure on the part of Christian husbands to think biblically, lead fairly, and release their wives unselfishly. Some women have every reason to be angry. Wife-battering is a favorite indoor sport. Faithful wives with no marketable skills are left with small children and never receive child-support payments.

3. A strong, well-organized movement to "liberate" today's woman . . . regardless. Even those who don't want to be "liberated" are made to appear foolish and backward. The fulfilled woman who enjoys being at home is mocked by the system.

4. An equally strong resistance from some voices in Christendom to keep the Christian woman boxed in, seated, and silent.

A Balanced Woman of God Sees . . .

Lydia: Acts 16:13-15
Eunice and Lois: II Timothy 1:3-5, 3:15
Philip's prophetic daughters: Acts 21:7-14

1) Scripture as God's vital and relevant Word, worth her attention, devotion, and application.
2) herself as valuable, gifted, responsible for her own growth and maturity . . . not overly dependent on anyone to get her through life or to make her secure.
3) the Lord as her strength, her refuge, and her shield when things refuse to be resolved.

A CHALLENGE TO MEN, A PRAYER FOR WOMEN

Chuck Swindoll offers:

> ### A Challenge to Men
> Why not ask your wife or perhaps your mother or sister the following questions to lend your support and help them sort things out?
>
> • What are some of the things you'd love to do—or become—as a woman that seem impossible right now? Be specific.
>
> • Am I sensitive to your needs? Are there areas where I could improve and give you renewed hope as a husband, son, brother, or friend?
>
> • What are some of your fears? Your hurts? Your frustrations?
>
> > FOR HUSBANDS ONLY:
> > • In your opinion, is my love freeing or smothering? Am I allowing you room and time to become the woman God would have you to be?
> >
> > • If something happened to me, how would you be able to go on? Are we being realistic with inevitable things that will impact our future, like the children leaving home or my dying prematurely?

> ### A Prayer for Women
> Dear Father,
> How difficult it is to trust You during times of trouble. This problem is magnified when many voices are telling us not to do this or to start doing that, all of which is counter to Your counsel. But they are close by and You, Lord, seem so far away at times . . . so slow to work . . . so terribly silent.
> Being a woman pulled in various directions is hard enough when things run smoothly. But it gets downright frightening when relationships are strained and our emotions within start screaming for attention. You know how we are, Lord! It seems like everything works against our feeling that we're worthwhile, valuable people. Our heads tell us, "Yes," but our hearts often say, "No."
> Do give us new measures of grace. And a vast amount of mercy. And Your matchless peace. May those special gifts free us from panic and get us in tune with Your Word so that everything false and phony will be filtered out as discernment replaces gullibility. . . . With quiet confidence, we trust You. In the name of Jesus, Amen.

LEISURE

Session 8

This [session] has one primary objective: to help you enjoy yourself, your life, and your Lord more . . . without feeling guilty or unspiritual! Yes, enjoy!

In our work-worshiping society, that is no small task. Many have cultivated such an unrealistic standard of high-level achievement that a neurotic compulsion to perform, to produce, to accomplish the maximum is now the rule rather than the exception. Enough is no longer enough.

Christians are not immune from stress fractures . . . how often have you heard someone boast about not having taken a vacation in several years? Or being too busy to have time to rest and repair?

Work is fast becoming the American Christian's major source of identity. The answer to most of our problems (we are told) is "work harder." And to add the ultimate pressure, "You aren't really serving the Lord unless you consistently push yourself to the point of fatigue." It's the old burn-out-rather-than-rust-out line.

This [session] offers a different rationale. It says not only, "It's okay to relax," but also, "It's essential!" Without encouraging an irresponsible mentality, it says, "You can have fun and still be efficient." In fact, you will be more efficient!

—Chuck Swindoll

YOU'RE AIMING TO . . .

■ Encourage group members to use leisure time better by understanding how we can imitate the way that God has modeled rest.

YOU'LL STUDY . . .

■ Selected verses in Genesis 1–3
■ Major themes from Chapter 8 of the book, *Stress Fractures*

YOU'LL NEED . . .

■ Copies of Resource 8A, "No Leisure in London"
■ Copies of Resource 8B, "Genesis-Style Leisure"
■ Pencils
■ Chalkboard and chalk or newsprint and markers
■ Copies of Resource 9B, "Pondering Our Final Destination" (optional)
■ Bibles

Step 1 (8-10 minutes)

Mouse Fever
Seeing the Need to Expand our Perspective in Life

Write this question on the chalkboard or newsprint:
What kind of _____-aholic are you?
Then pass out a copy of "No Leisure in London" (Resource 8A) to each group member. Have someone read the first section (three paragraphs) aloud.

Then present the question on the board in a rhetorical way. Add: **What is it you think about no matter where you are? What is it that prevents you from enjoying the things around you?** (Group members don't need to answer aloud.)

In this session, we're going to talk about how to relieve stress by including a godly amount of leisure in our lives. We'll look at the way God has modeled rest for us and how we can work this type of leisure into our lives.

Step 2 (5-7 minutes)

Leisure: What It Is and Isn't
Defining Leisure

Write the following sayings (from Chuck Swindoll's *Stress Fractures*) on the chalkboard or newsprint (if you have time, do this before the session):
"Fatigue is next to godliness."
"We worship our work, work at our play, and play at our worship."
"Leisure is not a take-it-or-leave-it luxury."
"The time you enjoy 'wasting' is not wasted time."
Which of these sayings is most thought-provoking to you or adds to ideas you already have?

Tell the person next to you which saying you chose and why. Take just a minute for each of you to share.

After allowing time for partners to talk, continue: **Most of us misunderstand leisure. Leisure is more than "time-off." Leisure is free activity; labor is compulsory activity. Leisure is doing things we like to do because we want to do them.**

Public Service Announcement
Examining How God Has Provided a Leisure Model

Chuck Swindoll notes that not one reference in the New Testament says (or even implies) that Jesus intensely labored to the point of emotional exhaustion. In fact, the Gospels record several times when Jesus deliberately took a break.

(If someone asks, refer to Matthew 12:15; 14:13; 15:21; Mark 3:7; Luke 5:16, 22:41; John 6:15; 11:54.)

God also modeled leisure for us in the book of Genesis as He took time to create, to rest, and to relate.

Pass out copies of "Genesis-Style Leisure" (Resource 8B) to group members who didn't get them last week—or who haven't brought their copies. Form three smaller groups and assign each group one of these topics:

1. Creativity;
2. Rest;
3. Relating to others.

Read the section that corresponds to your topic. As you come to a Scripture reference, have one group member look it up and read it to your group.

Then plan a three-minute presentation that resembles a television commercial or public service announcement on "Why Christians Ought to Create (or Rest or Relate)." Imagine that your presentation will be shown on a Christian television station. Do your best to present:

(a) how God modeled this activity; and

(b) how Christians can do this today. (Write instructions a and b on the chalkboard or newsprint, too.)

Use as much of Chuck Swindoll's material from the handout as you like. You may want to act out the Scripture itself or one of the anecdotes or something he suggests to do or not to do. You may use the board to draw a background or write statements on. You have only five minutes to plan your presentations, so read the material quickly.

Circulate among the groups, encouraging them to make their presentations energetically. After five minutes, ask the small group assigned to "Creativity" to begin. Pay attention to whether the group includes both points: how God modeled creativity in leisure and how Christians can imitate His example.

After the first presentation, thank the group. Read the "Creativity" portion of the handout. Then focus briefly on any points the group may have deleted, using the following information. Do the same with the other two groups and their topics.

Creativity

(a) God—Genesis 2:7 portrays God as a potter who "formed man of dust from the ground." (Jeremiah 18:6 states this comparison explicitly.)

Describing God at Creation, Swindoll says: "He mentally pictured vast expanses of land masses, deep oceans, colorful vegetation, an almost endless variety of living creatures . . . not to mention the stars, the planets, and the perfect motion of all. Finally, He creates mankind with a body and mind that still amazes students of physiology and psychology."

God enjoyed what He created, saying that it was good (Genesis 1:10, 12, 18, 21, 25). He delighted in His creation.

(b) Creating today—Time can fly when we're involved in creative activity that we love. It's as if we were created to create.

It's okay to delight in the things we create. Chuck Swindoll writes: "I must confess that occasionally I even say to myself, 'That's very good, Swindoll,' when I am pleased with something I've done. That isn't conceited pride. It's acknowledging in words the feelings of the heart."

When was the last time you looked at something and said, "Say, that's not bad!" (That's about as positive as we get with ourselves)?

What are some creative things you like to do that you haven't done for a long time or have always wanted to do? They don't have to be activities in which you create something out of nothing.

Later, the group will read the list from the lower portion of "No Leisure in London." Suggest some of the items from the list and ask for more ideas. Be sure to welcome all ideas, even if they may seem quaint or unusual to other group members.

For example, Chuck Swindoll says: "One of my most enjoyable leisure activities is writing—something I would never have thought possible twenty years ago. But now I realize I've had this itch inside me most of my life. It's such fun!"

A more unusual example: Karen had attended Bible college for a year and always wished she had studied Greek. After she married and had two small children, she bought a beginning Greek textbook. "I spend an hour a day and it's so rewarding. I feel like I'm accomplishing something tangible that I can use when I teach the Bible."

What's work to one person may be creative leisure to another.

Rest Time

(a) God—Swindoll comments further on God's Sabbath: "He 'blessed the seventh day and sanctified it,' (Genesis 2:3), something He did not do on the other six days. He marked this one day off as extremely special."

(b) Resting today—**What are some ways that you enjoy rest—perhaps even an active kind of rest?**

Physical rest: Imitating God in the strictest sense includes getting a full day's rest at least once a week. We should also get a good night's rest on a regular basis and snatch moments of rest throughout the week.

Devotional rest: Jesus often withdrew to lonely places and prayed (Luke 5:16). Even if we only grab "quick bites" for devotions during the week, we can take more time on weekends for extended prayer and Bible reading. Many people schedule regular times of contented aloneness (not loneliness) to think, to pray, to meditate. This builds us up spiritually and counteracts the stressful, frantic pace at which our culture moves.

Adventurous rest: People often find that adventurous or physically stressful activities are restful because they're such a change of pace. Many who engage in activities such as rock climbing, kayaking, or skydiving report that they return to their routines physically and psychologically energized.

What attitudes contribute to a lack of inner rest, to feelings of inner chaos? (Many of us impose unrealistic expectations or "floating guilt" on ourselves when we aren't "peak performers." Others of us have what Swindoll calls a "long-time 'heredity habit' of the all-work-and-no-play-will-make-me-happy philosophy of life.")

Our need for this kind of rest may explain why people in our culture spend

more money on recreation each year and manage to decrease their work week, yet still lack inner rest.

Relating to Others

(a) God—Why did God create us? Not because He needed us to work for Him. He created us just to be with us. In the same way, Jesus didn't need the disciples to support Him—yet He spent hours, days, months, and even years with them. They ate together and wept together, and they probably laughed together, too.

(b) Relating today—We need to value the relationships around us more.

How valuable are relationships to you? How much of your leisure have you spent developing and enjoying relationships?

How can relationships become more of a source of leisure in our lives? (We need to abandon the same influences that contribute to our lack of inner rest. Too often we compete with our friends and family members. When we get together with them, we try to impress them or prove something to them rather than to love them and be loved.)

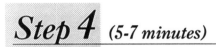 *Step 4* (*5-7 minutes*)

Toward a Life of Leisure

Stating Specific Ways We Can Incorporate Leisure into Our Lives

Ask group members to look once again at "No Leisure in London" (Resource 8A)—specifically at the lower portion, titled, "How to Get Started on Leisure." Ask them to read and respond to the suggestions (adapted from Chuck Swindoll's in *Stress Fractures*), adding others they may have.

Close in prayer, thanking God for His example of leisure and asking Him to help us imitate Him in this way.

Optional: Before group members leave, pass out copies of "Pondering Our Final Destination" (Resource 9B). Encourage them to read the sheet in preparation for the next session.

No Leisure in London

by Chuck Swindoll

Pussy-cat, pussy-cat, where have you been?
I've been to London to look at the queen.
Pussy-cat, pussy-cat, what did you there?
I frightened a little mouse under the chair.

Now there's a rhyme I'll never understand.
That little pussy-cat had the chance of her lifetime
. . . [to see] Westminster Abbey, Trafalgar Square,
Ten Downing Street. . . She probably didn't even
realize it was the historic Thames rushing by
beneath that huge rusty bridge she scampered
across, chasing more mice. After all, she didn't
even take the time to scope out the queen as Her Majesty walked across the courtyard. Not this
cat! She was such a mouseaholic that she couldn't break with the monotonous routine even when
she was on vacation. Same old grind . . . even in London. What a bore!

Can you imagine the scene as her husband met her at the plane back in New York? . . . "You
mean to tell me you spent ten whole days in London and all you can say for it is this stuff about
mice?"

How to Get Started on Leisure

1. Deliberately stop being absorbed with the endless details of life.
One of those details is (fill in your own) _____.
2. Consciously start taking time for leisure.
Circle any of the following that you can see yourself doing more often:
Jog or start an exercise program
Buy a bicycle and pedal two or three miles each day
Play a record or compact disc of your favorite music and lie down flat on your back, drinking
in the sounds
Enroll in a local class and take a stab at painting
Make something out of wood, do stonework around the house
Take a gourmet cooking class
Quilt or crochet or knit
Spend time at the library and pick up several good books . . . then sit back, munch on an
apple, and read, read, read
Plan a camping trip and spend a night or two out under the stars
Pull out all those old snapshots, sort them, and put them into albums
Work with house plants; do gardening and landscaping
Write some poetry
Don't miss the sunrises and sunsets, or the smells along with the sights.
Other: _____

GENESIS-STYLE LEISURE

by Chuck Swindoll

CREATIVITY

God begins with that which is "formless and void" (Genesis 1:2), lacking meaning, beauty, and purpose. . . . He added the music, harmony, and rhythm of movement—the miracle of birth and growth, the full spectrum of colors, sights, and sounds. He cared about details—from snowflakes to butterfly wings, from pansy petals to the bones of bodies, from the microscopic world of biology to the telescopic world of astronomy. . . .

You can write things with your pen . . . or paint things with your brush . . . or compose things, using your piano or guitar or harmonica. You can dream things with your mind and then try to invent them or draw them or in other ways bring them to reality through some creativity process.
. . .

God made things, then said, "That's good." [Genesis 1:10, 12, 18, 21, 25] After the sixth day, His evaluation increased to, "That's very good." [Genesis 1:31] . . .

Most of us are good at criticizing ourselves and finding fault with what we have done or failed to do. . . . The Lord knows that we hear more than enough internal put-downs!

REST TIME

Following the sixth day of creation, the Lord God deliberately stopped working. [Genesis 2:1-3] . . . It certainly wasn't because He was exhausted. Omnipotence never gets tired! He hadn't run out of ideas, for omniscience knows no mental limitations. He could easily have made more worlds, created an infinite number of other forms of life, and provided multiple millions of galaxies beyond what He did.

Several things contribute to our lack of inner rest: a poorly developed sense of humor; . . . our strong tendency to compete and compare, leading to a wholesale dissatisfaction with things as they are; . . . preoccupation with always wanting more. . . .

RELATING TO OTHERS

After God made man, He observed a . . . nagging loneliness that Adam couldn't shake. [Genesis 2:18, 21-22]. Later we read that the Lord came to relate to His creatures "in the cool of the day" [Genesis 3:8]. . . . the Creator-God took time to relate with His friends in the Garden of Eden.

Leisure includes times of communicating with others . . . [but we get] caught in the undertow of too many commitments. . . . Some time back our daughter . . . wanted to tell me about something important. . . . She hurriedly began, "Daddy-I-wanna-tell-you-somethin'-and-I'll-tell-you-really-fast."

Suddenly realizing her frustration, I answered, "Honey, you can tell me. . . . Say it slowly."

I'll never forget her answer: "Then listen slowly."

I had taken no time for leisure. . . .

Unless we are careful, the speed of our lives will reduce our communication to grunts, frowns, stares, and unspoken assumptions.

YOUR FINAL DESTINATION

Most of us don't like to contemplate subjects like death—or life after death—until circumstances grab us by the collar and force us to stare the questions in the face.

We lose a close friend, a spouse, a parent, a child . . . and suddenly life-and-death issues no longer seem vague and foggy. Suddenly, they are very real and must somehow be dealt with.

. . . Suddenly, issues like "eternal destiny" snap into sharp focus. Suddenly questions about our soul and salvation seem incredibly relevant. Questions we once hesitated to ponder or voice now cry out to be answered . . . [such as] "Is there some way I can be certain that I will go to heaven?" . . . They are good questions that deserve an answer.

. . . This is not something that calls for a lot of opinions. Theological double-talk will do nothing to mend the deep stress fractures we feel. The insights must come from the Bible, and they need to be so clear that anybody can understand them. They also have to make sense.

[This session addresses the] scriptural, simple, sensible answer for those who wonder about the single most significant subject in all of life: salvation.

—Chuck Swindoll

YOU'RE AIMING TO . . .
- ■ Review the plan of salvation to reassure Christians and to provide insight for non-Christians.

YOU'LL STUDY . . .
- ■ Matthew 25:41, 42; Luke 16:19-31; John 14:1-3; Romans 3:10-18; II Corinthians 5:21; Ephesians 2:8, 9; Hebrews 9:27; I John 1:9; Revelation 21:1-6
- ■ Major themes from Chapter 9 of the book, *Stress Fractures*

YOU'LL NEED . . .
- ■ Copies of Resource 9A, "Foot-in-Mouth Friends"
- ■ Copies of Resource 9B, "Pondering Our Final Destination"
- ■ Pencils, colored pens, construction paper
- ■ Chalkboard and chalk or newsprint and marker
- ■ A few Gospel tracts (optional)
- ■ Copies of Resource 10B, "Casting Out Demons" (optional)
- ■ Bibles

Step 1 (5-7 minutes)

Crisis Questions
Seeing How People Turn to Spiritual Issues in Time of Crisis

Pass out copies of "Foot-in-Mouth Friends" (Resource 9A) to group members. **In times of death or other crises, our thoughts sometimes wander from the crisis at hand to questions about our eternal destiny. We may have doubts about our salvation or about heavenly realities. But we're hesitant to say them out loud because we're afraid people won't understand the depth of our feeling. Some people may laugh off our questions; others give us simplistic answers.**

What are some inadequate or unfeeling answers the friends of these two people, Dennis and Maggie, could give them?

Read the anecdotes at the top of the page together. Encourage a wide range of answers. You may want to give them a few examples to get them started. (Flip: "Don't ask me—I'm not a pastor"; simplistic: "Here's a Bible verse—read it now and claim it"; well-meaning: "You've always been a good person—what do you have to worry about?")

In this session, we're going to talk about the doubts that we have about salvation and eternal questions and the stress that these doubts create. This can be a time for you to work through these doubts yourself, or to think of ways to help family and friends who are working through them.

Step 2 (5-7 minutes)

Destiny Doubts
Naming Doubts that People Have Regarding Salvation

Write these two questions side by side on the chalkboard or newsprint:
1. How can I be sure this is how salvation works?
2. How can I be sure I'm saved?

These are two categories of doubts that Dennis and Maggie had. They wondered if salvation and all the things they'd heard about it were real. (Even Dennis, a longtime Christian, had doubts.) They wondered if they could experience salvation and life in heaven with God.

Let's name specific doubts that fit under these two categories. Don't be afraid to suggest something that may sound outrageous to another. To simplify this, let's assume the doubter has a belief in God and at least a limited belief in the truth of the Bible.

Write people's suggestions under each heading on the board. (You may wish to ask a recorder to write them so you'll be more free to call on group members.) Possible suggestions:

1. How can I be sure this is how salvation works?
• Doubting the reality of heaven;

- Declaring that God will be a "nice guy" and let everybody into heaven (this is called universalism);
- Doubting the reality of hell;
- Preferring to think that God will not punish those who don't accept Christ, but that they will simply cease to exist (this is called annihilation);
- The plan of salvation seems too easy—a "free lunch" is never what it seems to be.

2. How can I be sure I'm saved?

- I'm not good enough because I've never done anything outstanding for God;
- I've done too many terrible things (this usually indicates guilt over a sin that the person doesn't feel forgiven for);
- Maybe I didn't say the right words or believe exactly the right thing.

As the group makes suggestions, combine any doubts that overlap and then number them to make it easier for people to refer to them in the next step.

Step 3 (25-30 minutes)

Questions that Count
Examining Doubts and How They Can Be Resolved

Distribute colored pens and paper and explain: **Use these to make a tract—a brochure-like booklet—to answer one of the doubts we've listed.**

First, choose one of the doubts on the board that you would like to make your tract about. If you need help finding Scripture concerning that doubt, see the "Scripture Resource List" on "Foot-in-Mouth Friends" (Resource 9A). Then think of what you can include in the tract to first capture readers' attention and then to inform them of how to resolve their doubts.

In the tract, you may wish also to challenge non-Christians to accept Christ or to reassure Christians of their salvation.

If possible, display a Gospel tract or two to help group members see how tracts are designed. (One that addresses a single topic or question would be the best example.) Point out that tracts often have numbered steps, questions and answers, and drawings of people questioning or reacting. Encourage people to work with one or two others if they wish.

As group members work, circulate among them and offer help as needed. Some may use up a lot of time simply choosing a doubt. Help them do that quickly so they'll have time to make their tracts.

You might even say: **If you're not sure which doubt to pursue, look at the "Scripture Resource List" and see which question interests you. Don't get too elaborate; let's try to do this in ten minutes or less.**

After the allotted time, ask a few to share their tracts. If their tracts don't include key Scripture verses, you may want to read these verses after they share.

Here are some summary statements you may want to use for the passages on the Scripture Resource List:

I John 1:9—God doesn't require us to be perfect before He'll forgive us. We just have to confess our sin to be forgiven.

II Corinthians 5:21—Christ became sin so we could exchange our sin for Christ's righteousness. (The wording of this verse in *The Living Bible* is particularly enlightening.)

Ephesians 2:8, 9—God's grace (unearned favor) is so great that He gives salvation as a gift, a "free lunch," so to speak. The price is actually quite high, but Christ paid it already with His life. To be saved, people must accept the invitation by accepting Christ and trusting in Him.

Romans 3:10-18—No human truly obeys the Law in its fullest, with a completely righteous heart. Under the Ten Commandments, people had to keep sacrificing for sin. Jesus made that sacrifice once for all. (The wording of these verses in *The Living Bible* is helpful.)

Hebrews 9:27—After death comes judgment.

Luke 16:19-31—Jesus didn't describe this passage as fantasy. The scene is unpleasant, but real. Hell is far away from heaven (vs. 23), permanently removed by a "great chasm" (vs. 26). The rich man was desperately alone and unable to escape—"none [could] cross over" (vs. 26). Other passages describe hell as a place of weeping (Matthew 8:12), unquenchable fire (Mark 9:48), darkness (Revelation 9:2), and everlasting destruction (II Thessalonians 1:9).

Matthew 25:41, 42—Jesus didn't say that this passage was a parable either. It is a description of judgment.

John 14:1-3—Heaven is a prepared place. Referring to Revelation 21:1-6, Chuck Swindoll describes heaven: "a place of beauty, peace, constant health, and happiness, filled with people from all the earthly ages who have one thing in common: faith in the Lord Jesus Christ . . ."

Step 4 *(10-15 minutes)*

Benefits of the Doubt
Exploring How Doubts Can be Helpful, Instead of Stressful

It's helpful to examine our doubts in light of Scripture, but we may always have doubts to a certain extent. Heaven and hell are not places we can see or touch before death. That's why salvation does require an element of faith.

Pass out copies of "Pondering Our Final Destination" (Resource 9B) to group members who didn't get them last week—or who haven't brought their copies. Give them a minute to read the first section.

Why do you think God didn't give us more "proof" of life after death? (The rich man in Luke 16:19-31 asked practically the same question. He described what he thought would be the best way for keeping his brothers from a life of ruin: "If someone goes to them from the dead, they will repent!" [Luke 16:30]. The irony is that Jesus did come back from the dead, but people still didn't believe. No matter how much "proof" is produced, it's likely that some would always doubt.)

Is it wrong to have doubts? (Doubting is normal. Working through doubts helps us develop our faith. When we are too lazy to work through them, our faith grows cold.)

Will we always have some doubts? (Experiences differ from person to person, but most Christians seem to research a question and settle it for a while. Then perhaps later, they deal with it at a deeper level. This is not bad. This is how faith develops and deepens.)

What kinds of problems or stresses occur when we don't investigate doubts about our salvation and work through them?

You may want to point out the following possibilities:

1. Self-righteousness. We subconsciously think that we must "be good" to be saved. So we try hard to "be a good person," even though we can't do that on our own.

2. Resentment. We may come to resent God for hanging this "heaven or hell threat" over our heads. We avoid God and spiritual issues.

3. Inadequacy. We feel so undeserving before God because of our sin that we don't "draw near to God with confidence" (Hebrews 4:16) in prayer; we remain timid in witnessing; we don't ask for God's power to overcome temptation.

4. Spiritual Mediocrity. Since we don't ponder the greatness of our salvation, we don't become truly grateful to God for it. As a result, our relationship with God is shallower than it could be.

Step 5 *(3-5 minutes)*

Thank You Notes
Thanking God for His Offer of Salvation

Thinking about the reality of life beyond the grave makes each of us ponder our eternal destination. It puts our earthly goals, relationships, and possessions, as wonderful as they are, in perspective.

Direct group members' attention to the lower portion of Resource 9B ("Pondering Our Final Destination") and have someone read it. Ask that person to pause just before the prayer at the end of the sheet.

This is a prayer that Chuck Swindoll wrote, thanking God for giving him salvation. After we read this together, please turn the page over and write your own prayer of thanks to God.

Ask the reader to continue.

Optional: Before group members leave, pass out copies of "Casting Out Demons" (Resource 10B). Encourage them to read the sheet in preparation for the next session.

FOOT-IN-MOUTH FRIENDS

Dennis accepted Christ many years ago. At the funeral of his father (who was also a Christian) Dennis finds himself distracted from the ceremonies and even his own grief. *Where is Dad now?* Dennis is wondering. *Is he really with God? Will I really be with God after I die?*

Maggie, on the other hand, has not accepted Christ. She attends church off and on, but is particularly anxious to go back this Sunday. Her best friend, Helen, has cancer; Maggie has spent several days with her at the hospital. *Is there more than this life?* Maggie is wondering. *Helen's body seemed fine, but now she may die. If she dies, is that it? Will I see her again after she dies?*

If you were a friend of Dennis or Maggie, what *inappropriate* comments would you be sure *not* to make if they shared the above with you?

SCRIPTURE RESOURCE LIST

What is required for God's forgiveness for sin? I John 1:9

How can anyone be "good enough" to be saved? II Corinthians 5:21; Ephesians 2:8, 9

Can't I be saved if I just obey the Ten Commandments? Romans 3:10-18

Is there really life after death? Hebrews 9:27

Is there really a hell? Won't God just annihilate those who go there? Luke 16:19-31

Won't God give in and let everyone into heaven? Matthew 25:41, 42

What is heaven like? John 14:1-3

PONDERING OUR FINAL DESTINATION

by Chuck Swindoll

Picture a person helplessly trapped on the sixth floor of a burning hotel. The elevators no longer function, the stairways are flaming infernos. To live, the person must leap into a net which firemen down below are holding ready. Imagine the trapped man screaming from his broken window, "I will not jump until you give me a satisfactory explanation of several things: (1) How did this fire get started? (2) Why has it spread so quickly? (3) What happened to the sprinkler system? and (4) How do I know for sure that net will hold me? Until you guys can come up with some pretty substantial answers, I'm staying right here in Room 612!"

. . . Slice it up and analyze it any way you wish, when we reduce our response to God's offer of salvation, it comes down to faith: being willing to abandon oneself, without reservation, to the eternal net God has spread . . . leaping while believing with absolute confidence that He will do as He promised.

* * * * *

[A young man] was looking at a large estate one day and said to a friend, "Oh, if I were lucky enough to call this estate mine, I should be a happy fellow. It's worth a quarter million."

"And then?" said the friend.

"Why, then I'd pull down the old house and build a mansion, have lots of friends around me, get married, have several fine cars and keep the finest horses and dogs in the country."

"And then?"

"Then I would hunt, and ride, and fish, and keep open house, and enjoy life gloriously."

"And then?"

"Why, then I suppose like other people, I should grow old and not care so much for these things."

"And then?"

"Why in the course of nature I should die."

"And then?"

"Oh, brother . . . you and your 'and then.' I have no time for you now!"

Years later the friend was surprised to hear from him, "God bless you. I owe my happiness to you."

"How?"

"By two words asked at the right time—'And then?'"

[from *Man: Ruined and Restored* by Leslie B. Flynn (Victor Books)]

. . . Loving God, thank You for accepting me and forgiving me many years ago when I was lost, and afraid, and confused and so far away from You. I am thankful that You heard my prayer and took me seriously, even though I did not know how to express my faith in Jesus very well. All I knew to do was to come as a little child, which I did. And You graciously took me in. Thank You for making it possible to KNOW eternal life with You—today.

OPPOSING THE DEVIL

Session 10

There are some stresses that go beyond the realm of the "natural." There are some pressures that cannot be explained in mere emotional or psychological terms. . . . People in the world may try to laugh it off, and people on the liberal fringes of Christendom may scoff or seek to explain it away . . . but demonism is neither funny nor phony.

It is real. It is, in fact, as serious and significant a subject as can ever be considered. But, strangely, it remains one of those unmentionables. Almost like, "Let's not talk about it, and maybe it will go away."

Even though we have ignored it, the world has exploited it. By twisting the truth and pushing the hot buttons of human curiosity and gross sensuality, slick promoters have turned it into a money-making extravaganza . . . a weird sideshow attraction with all the crowd-pleasing gimmicks. The last thing [the devil] wants is to have his presence and his strategy exposed.

Christians need to be informed of the truth: that we have the victory: that we are more than conquerors rather than helpless victims when it comes to dealing with Satan and his demons.

—Chuck Swindoll

YOU'RE AIMING TO . . .
■ Help group members deal with the stress of opposing the devil and his schemes.

YOU'LL STUDY . . .
■ James 4:7, Ephesians 6:10-18
■ Major themes from Chapter 10 of the book, *Stress Fractures*

YOU'LL NEED . . .
■ Copies of Resource 10A, "The Resistance"
■ Copies of Resource 10B, "Casting Out Demons"
■ Pencils and paper
■ Chalkboard and chalk or newsprint and marker
■ Copies of Resource 11A, "When Everything Has Been Cut Away" (optional)
■ Bibles

What You Don't Know Can Hurt You

Seeing that Ignorance Is Not Bliss

Can you think of a time when you didn't know something that everyone else seemed to? See if you know what these people didn't.

Mr. Y didn't know that putting cold water in his overheated radiator could _____.

Mrs. Z didn't realize that cleaning with ammonia in a closed room could _____.

(Suggested answers: Crack the radiator; cause Mrs. Z to pass out from inhaling the ammonia fumes.)

What fact have you not known that has caused trouble for you? Perhaps you've felt foolish because you weren't taught certain manners; or you weren't aware of developments in a certain person's life and said something that hurt the person's feelings. (Allow just a few group members to answer, then move on.)

In this session, we're going to talk about a kind of stress that many people—including Christians—don't want to understand or study. The topic is opposing the devil—resisting his schemes and battling demonic influence. Why do you think Christians in our culture generally don't discuss this subject? (Some are afraid; others may feel too sophisticated to believe in this "comic book" stuff and say it doesn't exist anymore; still others have known Christians that talk too much about the topic, claiming that someone is "possessed by the demon of nailbiting," for example. This last extreme is illustrated by the way even Jesus was accused of having a demon [Matthew 11:18]).

Chuck Swindoll talks about Satan and his stressful ways: "Some of you . . . are inexperienced and can only imagine what is involved in demonic oppression. Take it from me, it is horrible. It is ugly. It is vile. It is like nothing else you will ever encounter. It is exhausting and relentless. . . . Satan may be a defeated foe, but he won't give up without a struggle."

Why does Swindoll say that Satan is a "defeated foe"?

Point out that this concept is found in Scriptures such as I John 4:4 ("greater is He who is in you than he who is in the world") and Colossians 2:15 (speaking about Jesus' resurrection, Paul says, "When He [Jesus] had disarmed the rulers and authorities [creatures of darkness], He made a public display of them, having triumphed over them through Him").

Knowing about demonism does not hurt us because Satan is the victim; we are the victor. Being uninformed about demonic influence can make us the victim as it becomes an unidentified stress in our lives. If we don't understand how to resist the devil, we may continually get embroiled in spiritual defeat. If we don't recognize the evil one's influence in someone else (especially someone we love dearly), we aren't recognizing what kind of help the person really needs. Today we'll examine those two issues.

[Note: Christians disagree among themselves about some of the issues dealt with in this session. Feel free to use Chuck Swindoll's comments as a springboard for discussion, and to present your church's views as well if they differ.]

Step 2 *(10-15 minutes)*

Prescription Writers
Examining How to Resist the Devil

Let's first look at how the typical Christian can resist the devil. Turn to James 4:7 and Ephesians 6:10-18. Write these references on the chalkboard or newsprint and pass out paper and pencils at this point.

After reading these two passages, jot down a prescription for how a person can resist the devil. You may refer to other passages as well. Use language normally used in medical prescription writing—brief, directive, to the point. Try to include some specific steps. Keep in mind that Satan's preferred realm of operation is our minds. So he works through our thoughts, trying to become a persuasive force in our lives.

Circulate among group members, checking to see whether they have questions. (A typical prescription may include guidelines such as, get away from the situation [James 4:7]; stand up for truth and righteousness [Ephesians 6:14]; stay busy working for the cause of the gospel [Ephesians 6:15]; block Satan's doubts with faithful answers [Ephesians 6:16]; quote Scripture [Ephesians 6:17]; be sure your faith is in Christ [Ephesians 6:17]; pray in the Spirit at all times [Ephesians 6:18].)

Allow group members three to five minutes to work, but don't ask them to share their prescriptions. Refer them to Student Resource 10A, "The Resistance." Direct their attention to Part I, "Resisting the Devil."

This is a "prescription," so to speak, written by Chuck Swindoll after he studied the Scriptures, resisted the devil many times himself, and even witnessed the casting out of demons.

What items that you see here are included in your prescriptions?

Make sure that all of Swindoll's points are mentioned. You may want to note that the phrase, "Stand firm" appears three separate times in Ephesians 6:11, 13, 14.

Paul urged his readers to be confident and not budge because Jesus had proven Himself the champion no matter what kind of smokescreen the devil employed. Reflect a confident attitude to group members. Swindoll comments: "So whatever you do in dealing with demons, Christian, do it with confidence. With absolute, victorious assurance."

Notice how this process of resisting isn't filled with hocus-pocus or magic phrases. Resisting means to shove thoughts away, not to allow them to stay in our minds or enter them.

Serious Business

Examining What It Means to Be Demon Possessed

Chuck Swindoll explains in his book *Stress Fractures* **that the Bible doesn't use the terms demon "oppression" and demon "possession":** "The actual Greek text supports only the idea of being 'demonized,' which may include any one of several levels of activity and/or control. Sometimes the involvement was so deep that demons had to be expelled or exorcised from individuals. On other occasions, the person under attack was told to 'resist.'"

Pass out copies of "Casting Out Demons" (Resource 10B) to group members who didn't get them last week—or who haven't brought their copies.

Now that we have looked at resisting the devil, let's look at another level of satanic activity in people's lives. Let's imagine for a minute that you have been confronted by two Christians.

Christian #1 says, "I prayed while my pastor and others cast out a demon. If you know of anyone who needs that kind of help, give me a call."

Christian #2 says, "My pastor and my daughter's Christian therapist think my daughter is affected by demons somehow. I'm not going to let them near her. I know she isn't possessed—she's a Christian!"

Continue: **As we read this handout, underline phrases that could be important in answering these two people. Write in the margin a "1" or a "2" to indicate whether the phrases you underlined apply to Christian #1 or Christian #2.**

Then have volunteers take turns reading all of "Casting Out Demons" (Resource 10B) aloud. (If time permits, read Luke 8:26-33 as well after the first paragraph.)

After you've finished, ask group members to tell you which phrases they underlined. Here are some possibilities:

Christian #1. "Please proceed with caution. No one becomes an 'expert' in a deliverance ministry"; if Christian #1 seems too eager to find a demon-possessed person, you might underline: "We need to guard against witch-hunting. Some people see demons in most every area of weakness or wrong"; you might ask Christian #1 if he or she is still helping the person: "There must be follow-up support after the ordeal."

Christian #2. "The alien, wicked spirit certainly cannot claim 'ownership' of the Christian. . . . But while present within the body . . . , that evil force can work havoc within a person's life." "If a 'ground of entrance' has been granted the power of darkness (such as trafficking in the occult, a continual unforgiving spirit, a habitual state of carnality, etc.) the demon(s) sees this as a green light." "When people have become demonized, they need help—immediate, courageous, compassionate help."

Step 4 *(10-15 minutes)*

Fighting Back
Seeing How Resistance Works in a Christian's Life

Direct group members' attention once again to Resource 10A. Refer them to Part II, "Tale of the Resistance."

Let's work together to compose a story about someone who is resisting the devil. (This person is not demon possessed.) To make it easy, we'll use these unfinished sentences to guide us. Have the story come out so that the main character is successful in resisting the devil.

Use Chuck Swindoll's guidelines for ideas. If the group needs help completing the first sentence, suggest the word, "suicidal," or the phrase, "sorry for herself constantly because she lost her job."

After you've finished the story, remind group members that "successful" resistance must occur over and over. Successful resistance one day doesn't guarantee success the next.

Step 5 *(3-5 minutes)*

Building Up Our Resistance
Planning to Resist the Devil

On the board or newsprint, write the phrase, "I Need to Resist the Devil When . . . "

Ask people to mentally finish that sentence, filling in a situation that typically faces them with temptation.

Close in prayer, asking God's guidance as you and your group resist the devil and become more informed about his methods.

Optional: Before group members leave, pass out copies of "When Everything Has Been Cut Away" (Resource 11A). Encourage them to read the sheet in preparation for the next session.

If group members want to know more about today's subject, they may want to obtain these two books: *Demons in the World Today* by Merrill F. Unger, (Tyndale House Publishers), and *The Adversary* by Mark I. Bubeck (Moody Press).

THE RESISTANCE

Part I

Resisting the Devil

by Chuck Swindoll

1. Vocally declare your faith in the Lord Jesus Christ. Use His full title as you do this. Openly acknowledge that He is your Master, your Lord, and the One who has conquered all other powers at the cross.

2. Deny any and all allegiance to the devil, his demonic host, and the occult. Do this forcefully and boldly. Again, express these things aloud.

3. Claim the full armor of God, based on Ephesians 6:10-17, as your complete protection. Read the passage orally with emphasis.

4. Finally, state firmly your resistance of demonic influence. . . . Claim the promise of James 4:7 . . . he will flee from you.

(Excerpted by permission from *Stress Fractures*, © by Charles R. Swindoll, Inc., and published by Multnomah Press. This sheet may be reproduced for ministry purposes only.)

Part II

Tale of the Resistance

Maureen feels . . .

Yesterday she . . .

Then she called a Christian friend who said . . .

Maureen thought the friend was . . .

Maureen decided to use the tools mentioned in Ephesians 6:10-18 and began by . . .

She continued by . . .

She prayed that . . .

For several days Maureen continued to . . .

CASTING OUT DEMONS

by Chuck Swindoll

When one or more demons inhabit the body of an individual, that person finds himself under the control of the evil spirit(s). By temporarily blotting out his consciousness, the demon can speak and act through the victim, using him as his slave or tool. During such times (see Luke 8:26-33), the person often possesses incredible strength; a blasphemous, foul, vulgar tongue; a wild, violent temperament that goes to unbelievable extremes and frequently carries out dangerous actions against himself and others.

Scripture suggests resisting is something one does on his own, but when demons were actually expelled in biblical days, others were involved to assist in the process. . . . When people have become demonized, they need help—immediate, courageous, compassionate help. But . . . lest you allow idle curiosity to draw you into the idea that such a ministry would be fun and games, please proceed with caution. No one becomes an "expert" in a deliverance ministry. Our only ground of victory over evil power is our union with the Lord Jesus Christ.

Can Christians Be Demonized?

For a number of years, I questioned this, but I am now convinced it can occur. If a "ground of entrance" has been granted the power of darkness (such as trafficking in the occult, a continual unforgiving spirit, a habitual state of carnality, etc.) the demon(s) sees this as a green light—okay to proceed (II Corinthians 2:12-11; I Corinthians 5:1-5; Luke 22:31, 32).

. . . The believer has the Holy Spirit resident within. Therefore, the alien, wicked spirit certainly cannot claim "ownership" of the Christian. . . . But while present within the body . . . , that evil force can work havoc within a person's life, bringing the most extreme thoughts imaginable into his or her conscious awareness.

Demon Confrontation Today . . .

1. There must be a correct diagnosis. We need to guard against witch-hunting. Some people see demons in most every area of weakness or wrong. . . . Furthermore, there are characteristics among the mentally and emotionally disturbed that are bizarre, but not necessary demonic. . . . A reliable Christian therapist can be helpful.

Some of the things that might reveal demonism are: sudden and unreasonable changes of moods; aggressive, unrestrainable expressions of hostility; unnatural attachment to charms, fortune-telling, and involvement in the occult; extreme, enslaving habits of sexual immorality, perversions, gross blasphemy, and unashamed mockery.

2. There must be help provided the demonized person. . . . A careful study of Jesus' procedure is urged.

3. There must be follow-up support after the ordeal. A most vulnerable time occurs after the individual is relieved of demonism (Luke 11:24-26). Do not leave the individual without your assistance.

HOPE

Our bodies have been constructed to withstand an enormous amount of stress and pressure. God has made us to be fairly resilient people. We can survive the heat of the tropics or the icy winds of winter. With undaunted courage, we can go through seasons of illness, financial reversals, domestic disappointments, unemployment, or the death of someone dear to us . . . if. If we don't lose the one essential ingredient.

Hope.

We can rebound against wind and weather, calamity and tragedy, disease and death, so long as we have our hope. We can live weeks without food, days without water, and even several minutes without air, but take away our hope and within only a few seconds, we toss in the towel!

Knowing that is true about His creatures, God calls hope the "anchor of the soul," the irreplaceable, irreducible source of determination.

Hope is the opposite of despair. When you accept the fact that sometimes seasons are dry and times are hard and that God is in control of both, you will discover a sense of divine refuge, because the hope then is in God and not in yourself.

—Chuck Swindoll

YOU'RE AIMING TO . . .
- Inspire group members to trust God as their anchor in even the most "hopeless" situations.

YOU'LL STUDY . . .
- Genesis 17:15-19, 18:9-12; Romans 4:18; Hebrews 6:19
- Major themes from Chapter 11 of the book, *Stress Fractures*

YOU'LL NEED . . .
- Copies of Resource 11A, "When Everything Has Been Cut Away"
- Copies of Resource 11B, "Hope against Hope"
- Pencils
- Chalkboard and chalk or newsprint and marker
- Copies of Resource 12B, "Some Often-Asked Questions" (optional)
- Bibles

Step 1 *(5-7 minutes)*

Hopeless Pictures
Exploring How Hopelessness Affects Us

Pass out copies of "When Everything Has Been Cut Away," Resource 11A, to group members who didn't get them last week—or who haven't brought their copies. Give them a minute to read the section above the asterisks.

Chuck Swindoll describes the kind of hopelessness this woman feels: "Doubts often steal into our thoughts like termites into a house. These termite-like thoughts eat away at our faith. Our house begins to lean. For some people it completely collapses."

The picture of termites eating at a house is one way to describe how hopelessness gradually consumes us. What other pictures could we use? (Some examples might be a skin rash that spreads slowly; the way old age creeps on you until one day you can hardly do a sit-up and you say, "What happened?"; the way a pleasing melody gets fainter until it's gone.)

In this session, we're going to talk about having hope in hopeless situations. This is difficult to do, but it makes our faith grow and it also eliminates some of the stress we feel.

Step 2 *(20-25 minutes)*

A Hero with Hope
Examining How Abraham Didn't Lose Hope

Before the session, write the following references on the chalkboard or newsprint: Genesis 17:15-19; 18:9-12.

Today we'll be reading the Scripture as if it were a script. We need four volunteers to read the parts of:
- **The narrator (who reads all the parts that aren't in quotation marks, including "then God said . . .");**
- **Abraham;**
- **God (this part also includes the three angels as a group and the one angel who speaks—"they" and "he" in 18:9, 10); and**
- **Sarah, Abraham's wife.**

You may wish to list the characters on the board with these verse references:
Narrator: 17:15, 17-19; 18:9-12
God: 17:15, 16, 19; 18:9, 10
Abraham: 17:17, 18; 18:9
Sarah: 18:12
Pass out copies of "Hope against Hope" (Resource 11B) to group members.
Refer to the time line on the top portion of the handout and give a brief background.
Abraham and Sarah were 75 and 65 when we read about them in Genesis 12:1-9. This is the first point on the timeline. Sarah was "barren," meaning

that she had never been able to have children. At 65, she was also too old.

At this point, God established a covenant with Abraham. Part of it promised that Abraham would have an heir, a son. Then nothing happened. God made the promise again, which is shown at the next point on the time line. But nothing happened again.

Finally, after ten years, Abraham and Sarah took matters into their own hands. Abraham conceived a child with Sarah's maid, Hagar. This is the third point on the time line. Abraham and Hagar's child was named Ishmael.

Have the "script readers" read their parts in Genesis 17:15-19. Ask other group members to follow along.

This scene occurred at the fifth point of the time line. How long had Sarah and Abraham waited to have a child? (Twenty-four years.)

Would you describe Abraham as completely faithful and hopeful in the passage? (His laughter seemed to be one of doubt. Even after God promised that he would have a son, Abraham said, "Oh that Ishmael might live before Thee!" He still wanted Ishmael to be the heir.)

How would you have felt if you were Abraham, finding out that your plan to use Ishmael as an heir didn't work? (Sad for Ishmael—wondering what would happen to him; confused—Abraham thought he'd solved the problem; even more confused—wondering how someone as old as Sarah could carry a child.)

Have the script readers read Genesis 18:9-12 as other group members follow along. Then ask: **How was God's promise more specific this time?** (God named His timetable—the child would be born in the next year.)

Would you describe Abraham and Sarah as more faithful and hopeful in light of God's specific statement? (Not necessarily. Sarah laughed. This was apparently a laugh of doubt because God responded with, "Is anything too difficult for the Lord?" [vs. 14]).

The title of this time line, "Hope against Hope," is taken from Romans 4:18. These words were used to describe Abraham. Why are they appropriate? (As Abraham waited such a long time, he hoped when nothing made sense, when what God promised seemed physically impossible.)

It's interesting that even with Abraham's and Sarah's doubts, they were considered by Paul as being faithful as having hope against hope. What does this tell us about faith and hope? (God doesn't demand perfect faith that never has doubts in order to consider someone faithful.)

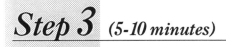 *Step 3* (5-10 minutes)

When Hopelessness Sets In
Examining Stressful Events that Bring on Hopelessness

Direct group members' attention to the statements under the heading, "Stressful, Hopeless Moments" (lower section) on the handout, "Hope against Hope" (Resource 11B).

We are most vulnerable to hopelessness in the three circumstances listed

here. Number 1 creeps in when we pray that something won't happen, but it does. This could be a loss of a job, a failure, or a death.

Number 2 occurs when we pray for something to happen, but the door is shut. This could be missing promotions, waiting to have children, finding the "perfect" church, house, or job.

Number 3 occurs when we pray and wait much longer than we expected, maybe years, until what we asked for comes to pass.

Which of these hopeless moments describes what Abraham and Sarah went through as they waited for Isaac to be born? (Number 3—they waited much longer than he expected.)

Which one describes their predicament as they saw that Ishmael would not be the heir to all that God had promised? (Number 2—they expected God to say yes, but He said no.)

Step 4 *(15-20 minutes)*

When Logic Is Lost
Examining How We Find Hope When Logic Escapes Us

When we lose hope, our human logic isn't enough. That creates even more stress.

Chuck Swindoll tells the story of a woman whose young son died during surgery. Her pastor comforted her by saying that God let this happen to her because He knew she was strong enough to handle it. She concluded, "If only I was a weaker person, Robbie would still be alive."

When we lose hope, we lose our proper perspective of what God is like.

What other comments do people make when they feel hopeless? ("What did I do to deserve this?" "No one else can help me now." "My life is ruined forever.")

Swindoll comments: "The mystery is enormous. . . . If we could unravel it, why would we need faith? If [logic worked], all we'd really need is the answer in the back of the book and someone to point it out to us."

How can God be an anchor to hopeless people like the woman on the beach or the woman whose son died?

Note that God's character is our anchor, especially these characteristics:

• God loves us and delights in us no matter how hopeless life looks. ("For the Lord takes delight in his people . . ." [Psalm 149:4, NIV]).

• God will not abandon us. ("I will not leave you comfortless: I will come to you" [John 14:18, KJV]).

• God is ultimately just and fair, yet forbearing. ("He [God] did this [sacrificed Christ] to demonstrate his justice, because in his forbearance he had not left the sins committed beforehand unpunished" [Romans 3:25, NIV]).

• God has His own mysterious way of working out His will that can come out to our good when we cooperate. ("The thoughts of God no one knows except the Spirit of God" [I Corinthians 2:11]. "All things . . . work together for good . . ." [Romans 8:28]).

How is hope itself an anchor in the way that it steadies us?

As we cling to hope, we are helped in these three ways:

• We are less likely to react negatively by becoming depressed or lashing out at others. Negative reactions create further guilt and stress and make it even more difficult to be hopeful.

• We are more likely to think clearly enough to recognize the good things that are going on in our lives and be thankful.

• We keep the perspective that knowing Christ is the most important thing in our lives. We know that we have something that no one can take away from us.

Refer group members to Resource 11A, "When Everything Has Been Cut Away." Ask someone to read aloud the portion below the asterisks.

How was this woman helped? (She felt hope once again. She was still afraid and she still had doubts, which is reasonable. But she no longer intended to kill herself. She felt enough hope to go on living however long God intended.)

Step 5 *(3-5 minutes)*

Termite Antidote
Finding Personal Expressions for the Concept of Hope

At the beginning of the session, we came up with pictures for how hopelessness creeps up on us. Let's create some opposite pictures—ones of increasing hope—to counteract those. (Recall earlier word pictures from Step 1.) **For example, termites can be eliminated with an exterminator's wand—a symbol for hope. If we picture hopelessness as being tossed around in the sea, an anchor makes an excellent symbol.**

Allow group members a few minutes to make suggestions.

Then close in prayer, thanking God that He is a sturdy anchor in the storms of life (or use some of the word pictures group members suggested).

Optional: Before people leave, pass out copies of "Some Often-Asked Questions," (Resource 12B). Encourage them to read the sheet in preparation for the next session.

WHEN EVERYTHING HAS BEEN CUT AWAY

by Chuck Swindoll

Somewhere along our many miles of southern California shore-line walked a young, twenty-year-old woman with a terminally ill disease and a revolver in her hand.

She had called me late one evening. We talked for a long time. A troubled young woman, her mind was filled with doubts. She had advanced leukemia. The doctors told her she would not live much longer.

Her husband had left her. Her two-month-old daughter had recently died. Her best friend had been killed in an auto accident. Her life was broken. She'd run out of hope.

* * * * * * *

She and I spoke calmly and quietly about what was happening. I did a lot of listening. There were periods when there was silence on the phone for thirty to forty-five seconds. I didn't know where she was. . . . She was taking her husband's revolver and going out on the beach to finish it all. She asked me a lot of questions about suicide.

In what seemed an inappropriate moment . . . I felt peace, a total absence of panic. I had no fear that she would hang up and take her life. I simply spoke very, very quietly about her future. . . . about Christ and the hope He could provide. . . .

She had a friend who was a nurse, who . . . had given her a New Testament . . . the nurse—her closest friend—was the one who had been killed in the auto accident. She had nothing to cling to from that friendship but memories and this Testament. . .

[After reading it, she called back to say] "I decided . . . [to] give myself to Jesus Christ. I'm still afraid; I still have doubts. I still don't know what tomorrow's going to bring, but I want you to know that I have turned my life over to Jesus, and I'm trusting Him through this. He has given me new hope . . . the one thing I really needed."

HOPE AGAINST HOPE

(Romans 4:18)

Abraham's Age	Event Relating to the Promise	Genesis
75	Abraham is promised a child.	12:1-9
Exact age unknown	The promise is repeated.	15:4
86	Ishmael is born.	16:3
99	The promise is repeated.	17:1-21
Exact age unknown	The promise is repeated; a specific time is given.	18:9-15
100	Isaac is born.	21:1-7

Stressful, Hopeless Moments

1. When God allows something I was convinced He would not allow

2. When I expected God to say yes but He said no

3. When things I believe should happen now happen much later

GOD'S WILL

Session 12

For too many years Christians have relied on vague hunches and weird hocus-pocus to know God's will. The paths that lead to an understanding of His plan are strewn with the litter of confusion, mystery, frustration, guilt, superstition . . . and major stress fractures!

Long enough.

God isn't playing a guessing game with His people. His will for us is neither puzzling nor hidden within some deep, dark cave requiring magical words to let us in on the secret. No, nothing like that at all. He wants us to know and to do His will; therefore, He is actively engaged in the process of revealing it. Contrary to popular opinion, anyone who sincerely seeks His will can find it. . . .

He has given us all we need to know it: His Book, daily circumstances, His Holy Spirit to communicate with our inner spirit, and wise friends and counselors. . . . Many are in His will who think they are not, because they are so fulfilled and happy in life. Surprising to some, God's will is the most satisfying experience in all of life.

—Chuck Swindoll

YOU'RE AIMING TO . . .
■ Help group members discover biblical, sensible ways to determine God's will.

YOU'LL STUDY . . .
■ Psalm 119:105, 130; Philippians 2:12, 13; Proverbs 27:17, 19; Colossians 3:15
■ Major themes from Chapter 12 of the book, *Stress Fractures*

YOU'LL NEED . . .
■ Copies of Resource 12A, "Some Unbelievable Methods"
■ Copies of Resource 12B, "Some Often-Asked Questions"
■ Pencils and paper
■ Chalkboard and chalk or newsprint and marker
■ Copies of Resource 13B, "Feelings of Unworthiness" (optional)
■ Bibles

Second-Guessing God

Looking at Odd Ways to Guess What God's Will Is

Pass out copies of "Some Unbelievable Methods," Resource 12A, to group members. Have different people read the three anecdotes.

Then ask: **If you were desperate enough to seek God's will in one of these ways, which one might you try?** Be ready to share your own answer to get group members to talk, if necessary.

Do you think these people's decisions were probably in God's will after all? Why or why not?

(The lady had all the resources she needed; she really wanted to do it; no reason is given why she shouldn't. The pastor must have known he was being deceitful to buy a doctoral degree; he would have known that deceit wasn't within God's will, which is why he kept searching for a way to make it seem as if it were. The young Christian's decision is less clear; he needed to work through more sensible ways to choose a mission field. He needed to consider questions like these: Would the mission board approve him? Was his health suited to that climate? Did he have any affinity for that culture?)

In this session, we're going to look at how to take the mystery out of determining God's will. God doesn't hide His will in a digital clock or an empty gas tank. Those who follow these methods are prime candidates for stress fractures. They find themselves in situations that confuse and discourage them.

Stop, Look, and Listen

Examining Ways to Determine God's Will

Pass out paper and pencils.

Jot down two or three ways that you think are good methods to determine God's will. Give people just a minute or two. Encourage them not to regard this as an elaborate exercise, but to answer "off the tops of their heads."

If your answer involves the Bible, raise your hand. Call on two or three to read what they wrote.

Ask group members to turn their attention to the next portion of Resource 12A, "How Does God Make His Will Known?" Have someone read Psalm 119:105, 130.

Direct the group's attention to "Stop at the Scripture" and say: **Scripture provides both commands and principles. "Speed Limit 35" is a command. "Drive carefully" is a principle. "Abstain from sexual immorality" is a clear-cut command while "Be angry, and yet do not sin" is a broader principle that requires enough wisdom to know when to show righteous indignation and enough forgiveness not to hold a grudge. If we're wondering about an action that**

nciple, we know it is not God's will.

talk about the "Lord's leading" or something simi-
eers read their answers. Ask group members to look at
d Within" on the handout. Then ask someone to read Philippians 2:12,

Philippians 2:12, 13. **First, we must have the desire to obey. We**
tell us His will, but think, **"Anything but that, Lord!" We need**
obey.

Chuck Swindoll notes, **"There's the need to 'work out' or give**
ing our part with a sensitive spirit (fear and trembling). And
e promise [in vs. 13] that God will 'work in you' to accomplish
e remain alert to His working, paying close attention to doors
closes, He directs us into His will."** (These three points are high-
st three questions under "Look.")
e to read Colossians 3:15.

As Cliristians, we are to have peace "ruling" in our hearts. Peace "acts as
an umpire" within us. If we've made the wrong decision, we won't be at
peace. In that case, it may even be necessary to reverse our decision if possible, which is better than living out of God's will and without peace.

Which of your answers talk about getting input from others? Have two or
three volunteers read their answers. Ask group members to look at "Listen to the
Counsel of Qualified People" on the handout. Then ask someone to read Proverbs
27:17, 19.

One example of this is the way older women in God's family are told to
instruct and encourage younger women (Titus 2:3-5). All of us need counsel
at times. "Like a quarterback, facing fourth-and-one on the thirty-yard line,
who calls a time-out to consult with the coach, so must we," says Chuck
Swindoll. "God uses others to help us know His desires."

Step 3 *(5-15 minutes)*

Willful Questions
Examining Questions People Have about God's Will

Pass out copies of "Some Often-Asked Questions" (Resource 12B) to group members who didn't get them last week—or who haven't brought their copies. Ask group
members to read silently all of it except the last paragraph.

If time permits, apply Chuck Swindoll's questions to one or more of the opening
stories. **Think back to the lady who wanted to visit Israel in the story we read
at the beginning of our session. Which question(s) might she have wondered
about?** (Group members may have various opinions. Here are some suggested answers. The lady might have asked question #2: Her feelings were positive but she
didn't make her decision based on feelings alone. She also considered whether she had
the necessary money, time, and physical strength. #3: Perhaps she was in the will of
God but didn't know it. As a result, she felt she needed the 7:47 confirmation to go.)

Which question best applies to the pastor's dilemma? (#1: He must have realized that purchasing a doctoral degree is deceitful, yet he planned to do it anyway. #2: He felt that he wanted it so badly that being deceitful didn't matter.)

Which question best applies to the young Christian's decision? (#4: God may not be telling him specifically yet. He may need to listen to the counsel of others more or look within to see if God has placed the desired destination in his heart.)

Step 4 *(10-12 minutes)*

Moving Day?

Seeing How This Practice Works in Difficult-to-decide Situations

Ask the group to focus its attention again on "How Does God Make His Will Known?" on Resource 12A.

As I read the following situation, think of how the Stop, Look, and Listen questions could apply.

Chuck Swindoll tells a story about Family A and Family B who live in southern California. Both families have numerous friends, a good church, a nice home, and family roots nearby—but they're starting to hate the smog. The hurried pace, mixed with heavy traffic and too many people, is starting to take the fun out of life. They're both thinking about moving to Washington state. Family A moves; Family B doesn't. Both feel they've followed God's will.

Assuming that both families did follow God's will, what factors not mentioned in the story could have helped them know this?

Answers will vary, but here are some possibilities. You may want to read one to get the group thinking.

• Family A could have found that its life in that area was somehow harming the family, while living in Washington would not have. Then moving would have been obeying a scriptural principle of caring for one's family.

• Family A could have taken a vacation in Washington, during which one or both adults were offered a job or a ministry opportunity that they thought was wise to take. They could have also felt extraordinary peace about living near that job or ministry.

• A wise friend could have counseled Family A about a specific situation in Washington that would benefit the family.

After group members have suggested their ideas, read this conclusion: **As it actually happened, Family A moved because it had a child whose health was endangered by living in southern California, while Family B had three healthy children. Family B was also involved in a discipleship ministry in which it specifically felt God calling its members to work.**

How do guidelines such as these on Resource 12A help us relieve stress in determining God's will? (They allow us to fully consider an idea. The objective part of us can compare a decision with what the Bible says and the counsel of others. The subjective part of us is not pushed aside, however. We are encouraged to look within ourselves at our level of peace with God because of our decision. If a path we choose gives us too much stress, we are bound to reconsider our decision.)

Many situations such as this one are so subjective that issues become hazy. They require careful and honest listening to the Lord and honest discussion among all the people involved.

Step 5 *(10-12 minutes)*

Making God's Will My Will
Seeking God's Will in My Life in a Sensible Way

Ask group members to continue focusing on the lower portion of Resource 12A, "How Does God Make His Will Known?"

What decision is currently troubling you? In what situation is God's will eluding you?

Perhaps it concerns a business or job decision, financial pressures, schooling for your children, resolving problems of your past, or taking specific steps to get along with others. If you can't think of a decision you're presently facing, think of one you've already worked through.

Walk this problem through the first two steps only: Stop and Look. Take a few minutes to do this. Use this quiet time to turn the decision over in your mind so that possibilities that have eluded you in the past may come to mind.

Allow people a few minutes of quiet. Then say: **Tell someone else here today about your dilemma or decision. Listen to what that person says. Don't be concerned that this person may not be "qualified." You can always evaluate that later. Sometimes the thoughts of the most "unqualified" people can shed light on our dilemmas.**

After two or three minutes, explain that it's time to give the other partner a chance to share.

Close in prayer, asking God to give group members the guidance they need.

Optional: Before group members leave, pass out copies of "Feelings of Unworthiness" (Resource 13B). Encourage them to read the sheet in preparation for the next session.

SOME UNBELIEVABLE METHODS

by Chuck Swindoll

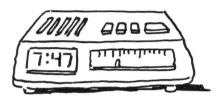

If we were looking for a new television series to amuse and entertain, we could name this one "That's Unbelievable!" Here are some examples we could feature on the show.

A lady received a brochure advertising a tour to Israel . . . her lifelong dream. . . . She had the money, the time, the interest, and the strength. But was it God's will? Before going to bed, she read the pamphlet once more and noticed that the airplane they would be traveling on was a 747 jumbo jet. After spending a sleepless night wrestling with all the pros and cons, she . . . knew it was God's will for her to go. . . . When she awoke and glanced at her digital clock, it read 7:47. That was her "sign" from God.

A pastor had served as a deacon in a former church prior to being called into the ministry. He toyed with the idea of buying a doctor of divinity degree from a degree mill. . . . He struggled with whether or not it was God's will. Late one afternoon, he stumbled across the answer he'd been looking for . . . : "For they that have used the office of a deacon well purchase to themselves a good degree . . ." (I Timothy 3:13, KJV)

. . . A young Christian struggled with the choice of his career. As he was driving and praying in Washington, D.C., he ran out of gas in front of the Philippine embassy. He got his answer. God wanted him to be a missionary and serve the Lord in the Philippines. (I wonder what this young man would do if he found himself suddenly stuck in an elevator with a young single woman named Mary. Would that be God's "sign" to marry her?)

HOW DOES GOD MAKE HIS WILL KNOWN?

Stop at the Scriptures
Psalm 119:105, 130
- Am I obeying God's commands? ("Abstain from sexual immorality" [I Thessalonians 4:3].)
- Am I obeying God's principles? ("Be angry, yet do not sin" [Ephesians 4:26].)

Look Around and Within
Philippians 2:12, 13; Colossians 3:15
- Do I want to obey it, no matter what?
- Am I being sensitive to what God is saying?
- Am I examining circumstances to see what God is "working out"?
- Has God given me an honest "peace" about a decision?

Listen to the Counsel of Qualified People
Proverbs 27:17, 19
- Am I seeking the counsel of wise persons?
- Am I following it?

SOME OFTEN-ASKED QUESTIONS

Resource 12B

by Chuck Swindoll

1. *What if I know the will of God but deliberately do not do it?* As in every area of life, when we don't play by the rules, we must pay the consequences. But consequences don't usually happen immediately. In fact, for a temporary period of time things may run along smoothly. . . .

Remember Jonah? He bought a ticket on the ship leaving for Tarshish and was even able to fall asleep. But by and by, he found himself in a threatening storm and finally in the belly of the fish. God brings discipline on His children. This includes external consequences as well as internal conflicts. . . . After [David's] disobedience connected with the Bathsheba affair, the man admits maximum misery within [Psalm 32:3, 4].

2. *Can't I rely on my feelings?* This is frequently asked with regard to things we really want to do—but which lack biblical support.

Take the case of a young woman madly in love. . . . She is a Christian, but he is not. Of course, he promises . . . he will not interfere with her interest in the Lord. . . . With all her heart, she believes he will someday change. . . .

But the Bible states unequivocally that to be unequally yoked with an unbeliever is NOT God's will, her feelings notwithstanding. Second Corinthians 6:14-18 and I Corinthians 7:39 are not eased by warm feelings and romantic moonlit nights. . . .

3. *Can I be in the will of God and not know it?* . . . I am of the opinion many Christians are! While it is true God desires us to be "filled with the knowledge of His will" (Colossians 1:9), many believers are not at that level of awareness. Furthermore, there is the weird yet popular idea that God's will is always something uncomfortable, painful, or unfulfilling. To some it is inconceivable that God's will could be enjoyable—even delightful. . . .

4. *What about specifics that aren't addressed in Scripture?* The Bible doesn't tell the Christian specifically where to live. Or which career to pursue. Or where to go to college. If it did, how easy it would be. Yet how little faith we would need!

. . . God gives us principles. He also moves and works through circumstances. He even "speaks" to us through the wise counsel of a friend. All of this keeps us trusting, depending, waiting, praying, reading His Word, and using healthy doses of common sense.

LIFE ASSURANCE

I've chosen to wrap up this book on stress fractures with one of the most encouraging, liberating truths in God's Word. I assure you, in all of life, there is no greater remedy for stress than a firm belief in the precious truth I will outline on the last few pages of this book. . . .

With feelings of fear and uncertainty while watching events from our windows, many of us often hear least what we need most: sound, reliable theology that offers reassurance and hope, based squarely on God's Word. Not feelings or opinions or even logic. We need to hear what God has said and rest our case there. . . .

Being . . . confident and comforted in . . . my salvation based on God's keeping power, not mine, [means that] all cause for anxiety is removed. I may tremble on the Rock, but the Rock never trembles under me! And that inner assurance not only relieves my fear, it allows me to carry on with much greater efficiency. Rather than causing me to be indifferent and irresponsible, it inspires me to direct all my energies toward those things that please and glorify the name of my heavenly Father.

—Chuck Swindoll

YOU'RE AIMING TO . . .
■ Help group members feel confident of God's love and His gift of salvation despite their sin, guilt, and doubts.

YOU'LL STUDY . . .
■ Matthew 11:28-30; Luke 15:11-24; Romans 5:8; 6:1-11; 8:1, 31-39; I Corinthians 11:30-32; Ephesians 2:8, 9; Hebrews 12:5-11; I John 1:9; Psalm 32:5
■ Major themes from Chapter 13 of the book, *Stress Fractures*

YOU'LL NEED . . .
■ Copies of Resource 13A, "Shaky Ground"
■ Copies of Resource 13B, "Feelings of Unworthiness"
■ Pencils
■ Chalkboard and chalk or newsprint and marker
■ Bibles

Step 1 *(5-7 minutes)*

Shaky Ground
Looking at Ways in Which We Feel Insecure

Pass out "Shaky Ground" (Resource 13A). Have the group look at the cartoon. **When have you identified with this man's insecurity? Perhaps you've started a new job. Or you have a new friend. You wonder, "How soon will I blow it?"**

Allow one or two group members to answer. You might have a story of your own on hand to get them going.

What kinds of situations usually make us feel insecure? (Situations in which we're new or we feel inadequate compared to the person we're with; situations which are important, so we feel we need to impress others.)

In this session we're going to talk about the importance of feeling confident in God's love and His gift of salvation. When we doubt that God loves us, we feel lost and inadequate. When we fear that God won't really save us after all, we feel panicky. We become stressed trying to do more or be more so that God will love us enough to save us.

Step 2 *(20-25 minutes)*

"Not Good Enough" Blues
Looking at the Bible's Answers to Our Insecurities

Form small groups. Direct people's attention to the four stories below the cartoon on "Shaky Ground" (Resource 13A). Assign a story to each group.

The people in these stories feel inadequate before God. They doubt that God loves them and they wonder if they're truly saved. Look up the Scripture that follows each story and talk about what a Christian friend might say to help this person resolve those feelings of inadequacy. Then choose two people out of your group to act out a conversation between the main character and the Christian friend for the entire group. (If no one in the group is willing to role-play, let people simply describe what they would say. The group working on the story titled, "But I'm not as good as . . . ," should choose one person in the story to focus on.)

Listen carefully to each group's presentation. Have groups read any listed Scripture verses that aren't included in their presentations. Thank each group and make the following comments as needed.

"But I still sin!" **Christ didn't wait to save each of us until we were "good enough." We received our salvation when we were sinners and we continue to receive it as sinners—only now we are sinners saved by grace. We do resist sinning (I John 3:6-9) because we love God, but salvation is God's gift.**

"But I'm not as good as . . ." **The people in this account feel "guilt by comparison." They have probably compared themselves with other Christians who seem to have perfect family lives and personal lives and concluded that they don't measure up. Yet Jesus called and loved people in all sorts of situations.**

One of Christ's longest recorded conversations was with a woman whose fractured life included five previous marriages (John 4:7-26). He never demanded perfection as a prerequisite for love. You might want to reread Romans 8:38, 39 and insert the phrase, "past or present relationships," before, "shall be able to separate us from the love of God . . ."

"But I feel so guilty about . . ." When the prodigal son returned, he was no less a son than when he left. The father didn't sit on the porch and growl at the boy; he ran down the road to meet him. In the same way, God is anxious to forgive. He asks only that we confess our sin.

"But I think I'm a 'carnal Christian.'" Jim is a lot like the driver who wants to see how close to the edge of the road he can drive without tumbling down the mountainside, instead of seeing how safely he can drive.

(If group members ask for a scriptural basis for "carnal Christians," refer them to I Corinthians 3:1-3, 12-14 and Galatians 5:16-23.)

Scripture does say that carnal Christians are disciplined by God. Says Chuck Swindoll, "According to I Corinthians 11:30-32, there were some believers in ancient Corinth who continued to live such carnal lives, God removed them from the earth. Yet even that discipline is not to be confused with condemnation."

In the same way, human parents discipline their straying children, but they don't disown them. Though this discipline can be unpleasant, it doesn't mean that God doesn't love us.

Step 3 (10-12 minutes)

Is God a Grouch?

Exploring Views of God

Write this phrase on the chalkboard: "If you emphasize God's love too much, people quit fearing God and don't try so hard to obey."

Some Christians don't want people to feel assured of God's love and grace because they're afraid these people will lapse into loose living. Or perhaps they'll become lazy and quit serving God. Can you think of comments, old sayings, or even interpretations of Scripture that express this idea?

(Comments: "Don't tell the preacher his sermon was good—he'll get a big head and quit trying." In "fire-escape Christianity," people emphasize hell to scare others into accepting and obeying Christ. Some parents have been encouraged to instill a fear of hell into their children to get them to obey.)

(Scripture: Some misinterpret the phrase, "Work out your salvation with fear and trembling" to mean that we should live in perpetual terror of God.)

In Romans 6:1-11, Paul answers the suggestion that God's grace and love is so great that people might as well keep sinning. "Are we to continue in sin so that grace might increase?" (vs. 1). Paul says that a transformation occurs ["consider yourselves to be dead to sin, but alive to God in Christ Jesus" vs. 11] in the Christian's life so that the Christian wants to obey.

It's true that fear sometimes motivates people to do better. But often it hinders their performance. Pass out copies of "Feelings of Unworthiness" (Resource 13B) to group members who didn't get them last week—or who haven't brought their copies. Read aloud the two paragraphs at the bottom and ask the group to follow along.

In the same way, our "spiritual productivity" grows as we feel confident in God's love and His willingness to work through us, imperfect servants that we are. When we live in constant fear of God's wrath, we aren't free to love him and serve Him. This doesn't mean, of course, that we shouldn't live in reverence and awe of God. But it's possible to do that and feel confident of His love, too.

Step 4 (10-15 minutes)

Feelings of Clay
Examining Why We Feel Unworthy

Ask people to read the top portion of "Feelings of Unworthiness" (Resource 13B). As they do so, write these two statements on the chalkboard:
"Feelings should be discarded."
"Confession removes our guilt."
Ask this question about each statement: **Is this what Chuck Swindoll said or implied in the excerpt on the sheet?** Use the following material for discussion.

"Feelings should be discarded"—(Feelings should be considered unreliable when they disagree with scriptural truths. We can feel that God doesn't love us even when He does. We may feel overwhelmed with guilt when God has actually forgiven us. But even when feelings are unreliable, simply discarding them doesn't usually work. Feelings are a God-given and important part of ourselves that have to be dealt with.)

How do we change our feelings—about guilt, about God's love, about feeling confident of our salvation?

Point out that David set a fine example in the Psalms of someone who spoke his feelings to God (even his unreliable feelings of revenge) and worked through them (see Psalms 64; 77). Meditating on passages such as the parable of the prodigal son (Luke 15:11-24) is helpful, too. We need to know in our hearts as well as our minds that God is like that forgiving father who accepts us back even though we don't deserve it.

"Confession removes our guilt"—(Psalm 32:5 [which Chuck Swindoll quoted] may seem to say that, but it is actually the blood of Jesus Christ that cleanses us. God asks that we confess our sin [I John 1:9] and promises to be faithful to forgive us.)

What is so powerful about confession? (It shows that we aren't pretending that we didn't sin, which is part of repentance. This honesty often helps to cleanse our conscience so we feel as if we can start over.)

What is false guilt? When do we feel false guilt? (It's feeling guilty for something for which we aren't to blame—or even for something we've already been forgiven for. It can be difficult to believe that God really does forgive us for so many things.)

Step 5 *(5-7 minutes)*

Imagine That!

Exploring How My Life Would Change If I Felt More Secure in God

Write this incomplete statement on the chalkboard:

"If I believed that God truly loved me no matter what and honored me as His child, I would . . ."

Remember how the workers on the Golden Gate Bridge worked faster when they had a safety net? As you become more confident of God's offer of salvation and His great love, you'll be more confident in obeying Him and serving Him, too.

As we close today, try to imagine how different you would feel if you felt completely assured of God's love. If you did, how would your life of obedience and service be more whole? More bold?

Write the end of the sentence on the chalkboard on the back of your handout. For example, would you:

- **Feel so fulfilled that you would reflect more love to your children?**
- **Have enough confidence to try to teach a Bible class?**
- **Be free to quit comparing yourself to "super-spiritual" people?**
- **Seriously consider going to the mission field?**

Close in prayer, thanking God for His great love and gift of salvation.

SHAKY GROUND

"What do you mean, 'I always bring my lawyer on the honeymoon, just in case'?"

"BUT I STILL SIN!"

"I don't understand how I can call myself a Christian," says Marilyn. "I still yell at my kids. I still let words slip that I shouldn't. I . . . Yes, I read the Bible when I can, but a Christian ought to do better than that." (Romans 5:8, Ephesians 2:8, 9)

"BUT I'M NOT AS GOOD AS . . ."

A whole pew of people at First Church feel like "second-class" Christians. The first woman is married to an unbeliever and he doesn't like for her to tithe. The woman next to her was raised in an abusive family and feels so depressed that she sees a counselor weekly. The man at the other end of the pew has kids on drugs, one of whom is in jail. (Matthew 11:28-30; Romans 8:31-39)

"BUT I DID THIS TERRIBLE THING."

Brent is glad to be back at church with his wife and children, but he also feels shame because he had an affair. He broke it off and he and his wife have gone to counseling. They are fully reconciled, but Brent can barely forgive himself. When the pastor talks about heaven and God's love, Brent thinks, *That's for everyone else, not me.* (Luke 15:11-24, I John 1:9)

"BUT I THINK I'M A 'CARNAL CHRISTIAN.'"

Jim isn't like all the other guys at church. His morals are a little "less cramped," as he puts it. He likes being in church when he's there, but he "doesn't make a big deal out of showing his face every Sunday." When he's feeling reflective, he remembers how much faith he felt back when he was in a college group and wonders if that will ever return. Sometimes he even wonders if he's still a Christian. (Romans 8:1; I Corinthians 11:30-32; Hebrews 12:5-11)

FEELINGS OF UNWORTHINESS

by Chuck Swindoll

Some days I do not "feel" married. But I am. There are days I do not "feel" like I am over fifty years old. But I am. And there are times I don't "feel" worthy of my family's love. But it is there in abundance. My feelings are often terribly unreliable. So are yours.

Remember the prodigal? After he came to his senses he returned to his dad and began his speech in all sincerity. And the son said to him, "Father, I have sinned against heaven and in your sight; I am no longer worthy to be called your son" (Luke 15:21).

But his faithful, gracious, forgiving, patient father interrupted that speech with sweeping actions of mercy and grace. He restored the worthless, undeserving, once-rebellious son to a place of significance in the family. Without reservation, the father hugged his son home . . . the same son who "felt" so unworthy.

Guilt does an awful number on us. It will lie to us and beat us into submission. It will convince us that God's promises really don't apply to us. It will yell so loudly we will mistake it for the voice of God. It will put us down, stomp on us, remove us from circulation, and create such deep stress fractures in our lives that we will begin to question our own sanity.

But the beauty of grace (our only permanent deliverance from guilt) is that it meets us where we are and gives us what we don't deserve.

"I acknowledged my sin to Thee, and my iniquity I did not hide; I said, 'I will confess my transgressions to the LORD'; and Thou didst forgive the guilt of my sin" (Psalm 32:5).

* * * * * * *

In 1937, the famous Golden Gate Bridge was completed. . . . During the process of constructing the first section of the bridge, very few safety devices were used, resulting in twenty-three accidental deaths as workers fell helplessly into the waters far below.

. . . An ingenious plan was arranged. The largest safety net in the world (it alone cost $100,000!) was made out of stout manila cordage and stretched out beneath the work crews. It proved to be an excellent investment in view of the fact that it saved the lives of at least ten men who fell into it without injury. Interestingly, the work went 25 percent faster, since the workers were relieved from the fear of falling to their deaths.

Want to publicize your course on *Stress Fractures*? Bring in additional group members by using these reproducible helps. Feel free to copy the bulletin insert below and the sign on the next page. Fill in the dates, time, location, and leader, and customize as you wish.

STRESS FRACTURES

Biblical Splints for Everyday Pressures

"Whoever dubbed our times 'The Aspirin Age' didn't miss it very far . . . there has never been a more stress-ridden society than ours.

". . . Add financial setbacks, failure at school, unanswered letters, obesity, loneliness, a ringing telephone, unplanned pregnancies, fear of cancer, misunderstanding, materialism, alcoholism, drugs and an occasional death; then subtract the support of the family unit, divide by dozens of opinions, multiply by 365 days a year, and you have the makings of madness! Stress has become a way of life; it is the rule rather than the exception."

—Chuck Swindoll in *Stress Fractures*

Want to know how to cope with stresses like unexpected crises, suffering, defiant attitudes, and resisting temptation? If so, you'll want to come and learn some biblical answers.

DATES:

TIME:

LOCATION:

LEADER:

This course is based on the book *Stress Fractures* by Charles R. Swindoll, published by Multnomah Press.

STRESS FRACTURES

Biblical Splints for Everyday Pressures

"Whoever dubbed our times 'The Aspirin Age' didn't miss it very far . . . there has never been a more stress-ridden society than ours.

". . . Add financial setbacks, failure at school, unanswered letters, obesity, loneliness, a ringing telephone, unplanned pregnancies, fear of cancer, misunderstanding, materialism, alcoholism, drugs and an occasional death; then subtract the support of the family unit, divide by dozens of opinions, multiply by 365 days a year, and you have the makings of madness! Stress has become a way of life; it is the rule rather than the exception."

—Chuck Swindoll in *Stress Fractures*

Want to know how to cope with stresses like unexpected crises, suffering, defiant attitudes, and resisting temptation? If so, you'll want to come and learn some biblical answers.

DATES:

TIME:

LOCATION:

LEADER:

This course is based on the book *Stress Fractures* by Charles R. Swindoll, published by Multnomah Press.

MULTNOMAH